"If you and your family are [...] your seat belts and begin *The Bible Ride*. It's an experience bound to entertain everyone—and guaranteed to bring fresh and practical insight to the Scriptures for young and old alike. This is the ride of a lifetime. Don't miss it!"

LES PARROTT III, PH.D.
AUTHOR OF *HIGH-MAINTENANCE RELATIONSHIPS*

"Gary Moon has written a terrific book. It's a gift to the heart and a gift to every family that wants to be shaped and molded by the ultimate 'book of values'."

JOHN ORTBERG
WILLOW CREEK COMMUNITY CHURCH

P.S. My eleven-year-old daughter read it and she loves it, too.

"Every family with young children will love *The Bible Ride*. Gary Moon's humor, creativity, and wisdom make Scripture come alive in ways that captivate children and adults alike. I heartily recommend this wonderful book!"

SANDRA D. WILSON, PH.D.
AUTHOR OF *RELEASED FROM SHAME*, AND
VISITING PROFESSOR, TRINITY EVANGELICAL DIVINITY SCHOOL
AND DENVER SEMINARY

THE BIBLE RIDE
BOOK 1

*Adventures that Bring
the Gospel to Life*

GARY W. MOON

Servant Publications

Ann Arbor, Michigan

© 1996 by Gary W. Moon

Vine Books is an imprint of Servant Publications especially designed to serve
evangelical Christians.

Unless otherwise indicated, Scripture quotations are from *THE MESSAGE*. © by
Eugene H. Peterson 1993, 1994, 1995. Used by permission of NavPress Publishing
Group.

Published by Servant Publications
P.O. Box 8617
Ann Arbor, Michigan 48107

Cover design and interior illustrations: Hile Illustration and Design, Ann Arbor, MI

96 97 98 99 00 10 9 8 7 6 5 4 3 2 1

Printed in the United States of America
ISBN 0-89283-980-5

LIBRARY OF CONGRESS CATALOGING-IN-PUBLICATION DATA

Moon, Gary W.
    Adventures that bring the Gospel to life / Gary W. Moon.
        p.   cm. —(the Bible ride. bk. 1)
    Includes bibliographical references.
    ISBN 0-89283-980-5
    1. Jesus Christ—Prayer-books and devotions—English.   2. Family—Prayer-
books and devotions—English.   I. Title.   II. Series.
BT306.5.M66   1996
249—dc20   96-9484
                                                                   CIP

DEDICATION

To Jesse and Jenna—who each contributed half a name for the creation of the lead character, Jesna.

To Regina my wife, who contributed half of Jesse and Jenna.

To my parents and the retired missionary, "Auntie," (who kept me during three formative years). Thanks for all the Bible stories.

HOW THIS BOOK CAME TO BE

I was brought up on Bible stories. More of them passed through me than cups of milk—which has proven providential to my cholesterol count.

In fact, I can't remember a single day while growing up that did not end with a family devotional. Always, as part of our devotions, one of my parents read a story from the Bible.

By the time I had a child of my own I realized the benefits of those family devotional times. So my wife and I brought home a colorful children's Bible story book even before we carted in the first carton of Pampers. And we didn't wait for any developmental milestones, like language development, before starting our own nightly reading ritual.

Time passed, however, and presented some obstacles. A second child was born, almost five years after the first.

While each passing December 31 would find us at a book store searching for another new Bible story book for the coming year, it became increasingly difficult to continue family devotions day after day. I think we once went until March 31. That was our all-time—post second child—record.

It seemed impossible to find a story book that captured the attention of our whole family. If it didn't bore the oldest it was sure to go over the head of the youngest, and if both Regina and I liked it, both kids were sure to hate it. I felt a lot like Goldilocks in search of the perfect porridge.

Then one day as the whole family was glued to the television watching a story about a Wookie and robots with alphabet names, it dawned on me. Princess Leia wasn't the only thing that was captured. So was everyone's attention. From young to old.

That was the start, but then later I was really pushed over the edge when I noticed all four of our attention spans attached to each word that fell from the mouth of a talking pig. It is possible to capture the attention of an entire family with a story.

Then one day at about this same time, I was blowing some dust off a book I had bought in seminary, but never read. It was titled *Synopsis of the Four Gospels* and was edited by Kurt Aland. I had purchased the volume because of the editor's considerable efforts in laying out all of the scenes of the four gospels in chronological order. But what caught my eye that day was the fact that there were 365 scenes recorded.

I knew I had seen that number before. It didn't take me long to remember that it was on the pages of a few million calendars, or to reason that it would be a wonderful idea to construct a family devotional book that went through the life of Jesus in one year.

So that was the initial impetus to construct a yearlong family devotional based on all of the scenes presented in the Gospels with each scene attempting to reflect the life of Jesus in a creative manner that captured the attention of the entire family.

The result is this book (volume one of the entire project) in which an ordinary, modern-day, TV-watching, church-going (on occasion) family takes a ride at an amusement park that takes them through all of the scenes of the gospels (the first segment is presented in this volume). The Pilgrim family becomes physically present to see, hear, feel, taste, and smell the Bible characters who are writing Scripture with their lives.

Their tour guide is a five-year-old child (who may well be an angel) and the narrator is the family pet (a deep-thinking dog, not a shallow pig).

In *The Bible Ride*, the attempt is made to write in a popcorn-broccoli style (i.e., fun to consume *and* good for you, too). At times the stories float on the winds of fiction, but there is a tight string of historical accuracy attached. The Scriptural references listed in the notes section for each "scene" and the scores of direct quotes from Scripture which are peppered throughout the text, firmly anchor the stories in biblical truth.

So, with that said, enjoy the ride. The brave of heart may even want to put their hands in the air as we twist, turn, and drop our way through the first ninety scenes of *The Bible Ride*.

GOOD NEWS FOR PILGRIMS

Hello there! If you've got a little time, I'd love to tell you about what happened to my family last week. We went on an incredible ride.

The family I want to tell you about is called the Pilgrims; they belong to me, I'm their dog. My name is Wisdom.

Just last Friday we were all at Daffy World. It's a special place where people go to be amused—and, can you believe it, it's an amusement park that allows *dogs*.

As you probably know, amusement parks have lots of rides, like roller coasters (which I can't ride because I'm not as tall as that little wooden girl's hand), plastic rivers, and haunted houses. But, what I liked best were all the interesting things to smell. And, let me tell you, there was more smelling than riding going on that day. The place was as packed as the space around a city fire hydrant.

Mostly, everyone was just standing in long lines, sweating a lot, and grumbling at each other. It was hot enough to make a pig sweat that day. Of course, pigs and dogs don't sweat.

I was spending my time trying to keep my tail out from under the Pilgrims' eight feet, and watching the herd of people—tall ones and short ones, skinny ones and fat ones, smelly ones and more smelly ones, and one that was almost as furry as me.

Every once in a while I would get pretty bored. When that happened I would try extra hard to attract their attention by wagging my tail against their ankles or pawing Pete. (He's the youngest and easiest to distract of the Pilgrims.) It didn't work. They were too busy being miserable, sweating and waiting in line to go with me to have some fun.

Well, after about a half-hour wait to ride "The Dragon Master," Mr. Pilgrim, he's the dad, had had about all the amusement he could stand. "We haven't moved thirty feet since we got in this line. What are the workers doing up there, taking a lunch hour at three in the afternoon?" he thundered.

"That reminds me, Dad," Pete said, "I'm getting kinda hungry." Mr. Pilgrim shot a disbelieving glare at Pete's cotton candy-stained face.

"Dad," said Priscilla, Pete's big sister, "If we've only gone thirty feet in thirty minutes then that's just one foot per minute. The way I calculate it, it will take us more than ten hours to get to the front of this line, assuming we are still over six hundred feet from the Dragon's mouth, which is what it appears to be."

"Dad," Pete said while he was tugging on his father's pants, "I can't wait ten hours to eat. I'm hungry right now!"

Pete's dad pried a sticky little hand away from his pants and scratched at the neon-pink cotton candy residue which Pete had left behind. But before Mr. Pilgrim answered him, Mrs. Pilgrim, she's the mom, tapped her husband on the shoulder and said, "Honey, let's get out of this line and go over to that one—no one's riding it right now."

"What!" said Mr. Pilgrim, "and waste the thirty minutes we've already spent in this line."

"Thirty-two minutes, Dad," Priscilla said, and she poked at the knobs on her watch.

"Yeah, Dad," said Pete. "Let's go ride that one. There's a frozen slushy stand on the way—and a bathroom! I can't wait much longer," he said as his legs made the letter X.

"But no one's in line for that one," Priscilla said. "That must mean it's a real dud. Besides, look what it's called, 'The Bible Ride.' Who would want to ride that?"

"I bet my Sunday school teacher would," said Pete.

"That's just my point." Priscilla didn't look too happy at the prospects of the ride.

"I kinda liked Bible school this summer," Pete said. "They had Kool-Aid and cookie breaks every day. Let's go get some. I mean, let's go ride that one."

"No!" yelped Priscilla. And she almost stomped out her exclamation point on my tail.

"It's probably air-conditioned in there," said Mrs. Pilgrim, with a let's-do-it lilt in her voice.

"Let's go then," said Mr. Pilgrim, just as a drop of sweat dove from the tip of his nose to the asphalt below. "We can always come back later and ride this one." And with that he grabbed both of his Pilgrim kids by their sticky hands, ducked under a metal bar, and began to march toward the opening of the Bible Ride.

"No, Pete!" he said and tightened his grip on Pete's hand as they passed the frozen slushy stand.

"But Daaaaad," Pete whined.

"Don't be such a pig," said Priscilla.

I just followed along, wagging and panting. The thought of air-conditioning sounded very fine to me.

Even a dog would have to admit that the entrance to the Bible Ride wasn't much to look at. There was no paint or polish, no glitz or glitter. We squeezed through a cross-shaped opening in a high wooden fence, and we were in.

We walked back and forth through a maze of metal rails just like we did at the other rides, except there was no one else waiting to get in. Soon we came to an oversized door.

Mr. Pilgrim grabbed the iron handle with both hands and pulled it open. A wave of cool air rushed out to meet us and parted the fur on my back. "Ah!" said all the Pilgrims at the same-time. "Air-conditioning!"

They all bolted through the door as one body with eight legs. I was lucky to get in with my tail still attached. Then, we all went through another maze of metal rails and arrived at another door. This one looked as if it were made of gold.

"That can't be real. Can it?" said Mrs. Pilgrim.

"No way!" said Priscilla, "Do you know how much a door that big, made out of gold, would cost?"

Pete groaned, "I'm sure you could figure it out, Spock, but why don't you spare us this time."

"Shhhh!" said Mr. Pilgrim, with his finger to his mouth. "That's no way to talk to your sister."

"This place is huge! I can't see the ceiling or even a wall," said Priscilla, leaning *way* back to look up.

"Yeah," said Pete. "It's so big we may not hear our echoes come back until tomorrow."

"I can't even figure out how much it would cost to air-condition this place" Priscilla said, as she rapidly poked at the knobs on her wrist computer. The other Pilgrims looked at her in disbelief, their mouths wide open.

Pete finally broke the silence. "If *you* can't figure it out, then it's HUGE!"

Just about that time the golden doors began to slowly part, gliding inward. Light poured out from the other side. After my eyes adjusted to the brightness, I made out the figure of a small child. She had golden hair and was wearing a white robe. Her face was angelic. I halfway expected to see wings sprouting out of her back. Or a halo. She had neither.

"Hello," she said with the sweet voice of a very young child. She bent down to pat me on the head. "Welcome to the Bible Ride. Come on in."

We all crept into the beam of light.

"My name is Jesna. I'll be your tour guide for this ride."

"Are you old enough to work here?" said Priscilla, her head tilted as she looked Jesna up and down.

"Is there a bathroom in here?" Pete asked before Jesna could answer.

Mr. Pilgrim didn't give Jesna a chance to answer either question. He dropped to his knees so he could look her right in the eyes. "Uh, I'm a little confused. I mean, where is everybody? This is pretty elaborate for so few people to be in line. In fact, we seem to be the whole line!"

"I'm five years old. There is no bathroom, but the ride is so short you won't need one. And, there aren't many people who want to go on this ride. But that's really sad. It's by far the most fun of all the rides in the park. And, I would love to be your host."

"Will we get wet?" said Pete.

"Yes," Jesna answered.

"Does it go real fast?" he followed.

"Oh yes!, sometimes faster than light."

"Wait a minute," said Priscilla. "How can there be water, and fast speeds, and the whole thing will be over before bladder-boy has to go to the bathroom? It's a scientific fact that nothing goes faster than light."

"What time do you have, Priscilla?" asked Jesna.

"It's exactly 1:30:01 P.M.," Priscilla said, as she pressed several buttons on her watch.

"We will be back to this point before your watch reads 1:31:00."

"Yeah, right!" said Priscilla. "We'll go on a ride and be back in 59 seconds."

"This I've got to see," Pete chimed in, "Let's do it!"

"Well," said their dad, "You've certainly got my curiosity up. And it is air-conditioned in here. Let's give it a whirl. That is, if it's OK with you, Dear?"

"I'm game," said Mrs. Pilgrim, "But, I don't know what can happen in sixty seconds."

"In sixty seconds," Jesna answered, as she looked at Priscilla with a kind smile, "light from the sun could make it about one-seventh of the way to earth, or God could make it to the end of his universe and back, a million times—it's long enough for your whole life to be turned upside-down and inside-out."

And with that, a metal car that looked like it was riding on a pocket of air pulled up beside them. "After you," said Jesna, motioning toward the car. Two doors on the side opened automatically.

The Pilgrims piled into the car and sat two each on the cushioned seats. I wiggled into a spot between Pete and Priscilla in the front seat. Jesna sat facing us on the hood of the car.

As our vehicle eased into motion again, Jesna handed us each a pair of dark glasses. "Here," she said. "You'll be needing these." There was even a long, skinny doggy-pair for me.

"Cool," said Pete, "3-D."

Jesna looked at him and giggled. "Not exactly. They're sunglasses. It's going to be pretty bright in there."

We turned a corner and passed through what appeared to be the eye of an oversized needle. We were on our way to a most excellent adventure.

SCENE ONE
AN EXPLOSION OF LIGHT[1]

 Our car moved slowly to the center of the giant, dome-shaped room. The top seemed as high as the sky itself, and it was so wide that even a greyhound wouldn't be able to run all the way across without stopping for a pant break.

"Better put your glasses on now," said Jesna, with a little urgency in her voice. Just then the room went pitch-black, I mean molasses-syrup-at-midnight black.

"This seems like a strange time to be putting on sunglasses," Priscilla declared, as she slid the thick rims onto her nose.

"Shhhh!" said Mrs. Pilgrim.

There were a few seconds of total silence. And then—the sounds and sights of a streaking, screaming, giant meteor-of-light split the darkness like a chain saw ripping through butter. Even wearing sunglasses I had to squint and look away.

The light crashed into our car. It was bright enough to tan their skins and bleach my fur, but it didn't. It made all the darkness run away and hide.

Everyone was thrown back against the seats in terror. Everyone except Jesna and Pete, that is.

"Wooooeee!" shouted Pete. "This is way cool."

No one else spoke. They had been struck dumb by the explosion of light. Then, a deep voice that sounded sort of like a holy Darth Vader, except deeper and richer, poured into the room in slow-moving waves. Here's what the voice said:

The Word was first,
the word present to God,
God present to the Word.
The Word was God,
in readiness for God from day one.
Everything was created through him;
nothing—not one thing!—
came into being without him.
What came into existence was Life,
and the Life was Light to live by.
The Life-Light blazed out of the darkness;
the darkness couldn't put it out....
The Life-Light was the real thing:
Every person entering Life
he brings into Light.
He was in the world
… and yet the world didn't even notice.
He came to his own people,
but they didn't want him.
But whoever did want him,
who believed he was who he claimed
and would do what he said,
He made to be their true selves,
their child-of-God selves.
These are the God-begotten,
not blood-begotten.[2]

There was a long silence. Then we all looked at Jesna.
"We're off," was all she said.

FAMILY DISCUSSION

1. What do you think it means to become your "child-of-God self"?

2. In what ways do you think people who have become their "child-of-God self" act differently than those who have not?

3. What do you need to do to become your child-of-God self?

SCENE TWO
THE PROMISE AND BIRTH OF JOHN THE BAPTIST[3]

And off we were! Our car started moving ahead, faster and faster, like a bobsled on greased ice. "Wooooo!" shouted all the Pilgrims except Pete.

He shouted "Waaaaahooooo!" and raised both hands over his head.

I think I was the first to see it. I know I was the first to let out a howl. Straight in front of us was a huge sandy-brown, rock-like structure with all kinds of people standing in front of it. It looked like they were all wearing dresses or bathrobes. Whatever they had on, we were racing right toward them and toward that big, rocky building that was right behind them.

"We're about to enter the Temple," Jesna said in a calm voice.

"No!" shouted Mr Pilgrim. "It's about to enter us!"

The Pilgrims screaming "Yaaiiiiiiiiiiii" made my own howl (it's a cat's worst nightmare) sound like a whisper. I closed my eyes. I didn't want to see the splatter.

Then, as suddenly as it had started, our car came to a stop. I opened my eyes and gazed at what appeared to be the inside of the huge square-of-rock that we should have smashed into. I don't know... it was all very confusing.

"What's going on here?" Mr. Pilgrim managed to mutter before his bottom jaw got so low it almost dropped into his knees.

"Where are we?" said Mrs Pilgrim.

"How did we get through that wall?" said Priscilla.

"This isn't Kansas anymore," Pete said.

"Nope," said Jesna. "We're smack-dab in the middle of the Temple in Jerusalem."

"My goodness!" exclaimed Mr. Pilgrim. "How do they make it look so real?"

"No, Mr. Pilgrim," said Jesna. "You don't get it. This is THE Temple in THE Jerusalem. It's around 15 months B.C."

"I'm sure!" said Priscilla with a smirk.

"I'm glad you are," said Jesna, not noticing that Priscilla's face was contorted by disbelief.

"Now shhhh," said Jesna, in her soft little voice. "Gabriel is about to speak."

We looked out from our car and saw an incredible sight. There, just a few feet in front of us, was an old man wearing a long white robe all decorated with tassels and bits of gold. He had on a big white hat that made me wonder if he were an over-dressed chef. The smoke that floated up from the table where he was working made me sure that was *exactly* what he was.

The odor, however, which rose with the smoke was very strange—spicy-sweet and pleasant—but it sure didn't smell like it was coming from anything that you could eat. It didn't even make my mouth water.

"That's Zachariah," Jesna told us. "He's a priest assigned to service in the regiment of Abijah."

"I think Abijah plays for the Knicks," Pete announced with a nod and a 'pretty-cool-huh?' look on his face.

"Zachariah is married to Elizabeth, and he is about to hear something very special from Gabriel."

"He's that old quarterback that used to play for the Rams, right?" Pete was on a roll.

"Nope", said Jesna. "Gabriel's not a quarterback, and he's still playing. Look up."

We all looked up… way up… and saw a man as big as a small silo. He was wearing a gown that appeared to be made out of light. He opened his mouth and this is what we heard.

"Don't fear, Zachariah." [and indeed, Zachariah looked like a cat staring at a Doberman]. "Your prayer has been heard. Elizabeth, your wife, will bear you a son…."

"Wooee!" exclaimed Pete.

"…You are to name him John. You're going to leap for joy like a gazelle, and not only you—many will delight in his birth. He'll achieve great stature with God….

"He will herald God's arrival in the style and strength of Elijah, soften the hearts of parents to children, and kindle devout understanding among hardened skeptics. He'll get the people ready for God."

"Wow!" said Mrs. Pilgrim, "This ride makes you feel like you are seeing things that happened in the Bible."

"Mrs. Pilgrim," Jesna interrupted in a soft whisper, "you are more right than you know. This *is* a ride through the Bible. That *is* Zachariah and Gabriel. And the noise you hear outside are the sounds of impatient Jews who are wondering what is keeping their priest. Like all of you, they don't have a clue about what just happened here. An angel has just announced the birth of a baby, a very special baby, the one who will prepare the way for their long-awaited Savior"

"To that old guy?" Pete asked.

"Yes," said Jesna, "To that old guy. Just like God sent a son to another old guy, Abraham, God is honoring Zachariah's faith (and the faith of his old wife) with a special gift."

"Holy smoke!" said Pete, as waves of incense floated past us.

"Exactly!" said Jesna.

FAMILY DISCUSSION

1. What do you think it means to have a "soft heart" instead of a "hard" one?

2. What would it feel like to have your heart softened?

3. Think about a difficult situation you have to face sometime next week. How will you handle it if your heart is soft?

SCENE THREE
THE ANNUNCIATION[4]

 I know you may think that I am crazy, but just before our car started moving again— and I am as sure about this as I am that fleas exist—that tall-as-an-oak-tree Gabriel looked at me and winked.

But, before I could reply with a polite bark, we were off again—slowly at first—right back through the walls of the temple. But then, with a flash of light and a sudden burst of speed that shoved our heads back against our seats, we were in a whole new place. Our car stopped just a few feet in front of a girl who was on her knees, talking and crying into her hands. "Shhhh," Mr. Pilgrim said to his crew. "Don't disturb her." "We could have hit her…" Pete managed before his father's large hand covered his mouth.

The girl looked to be about thirteen years old. She had thick, dark-brown hair, and was wearing a dust-covered beige robe. Her elbows were wet from the tears that were trickling down between her fingers.

She was all alone on the top of a small rocky knoll. It was early in the morning. Only half of the sun had squeezed up past the horizon. In the valley behind I could see the scattered lights of a small city that was beginning to wake up. It appeared to be a place where the Flintstones might live, except I didn't see any cars or drive-in movies.

The smells of burning wood and flowers floated on the cool morning air. Then, all of a sudden, Gabriel was back. I mean, BOOM! right out of nowhere, back.

The girl who was praying, or crying, had yet to see him as he started speaking to her.

> "Good morning!
> You're beautiful with God's beauty,
> Beautiful inside and out!
> God be with you."

The girl bolted straight up, scared out of her wits! Who wouldn't be if you were suddenly spoken to by a three-story beam of light? All four of my paws were shaking, and he wasn't even talking to me.

"Mary, you have nothing to fear. God has a surprise for you: You will become pregnant and give birth to a son and call his name Jesus."

Mr. Pilgrim looked at Priscilla and gulped so hard his Adam's apple slammed into his chin and made his eyes bulge. "She's so young," he whispered.

> "He will be great,
> be called 'Son of the Highest,'
> The Lord God will give him
> the throne of his father David;
> He will rule Jacob's house forever—
> no end, ever, to his kingdom."
> "But how?..." The angel answered,
> "The Holy Spirit will come upon you,
> the power of the Highest hover over you;
> Therefore, the child you bring to birth
> will be called the Holy, Son of God."

"She's going to have a little baby God?" The question burst from Pete.

"Whump!" went his dad's hand as it found its familiar resting place over Pete's mouth.

"That's exactly right," Jesna said.

Then Mary said:

> "Yes, I see it all now:
> I'm the Lord's maid, ready to serve.
> Let it be with me
> just as you say."[5]

Then Gabriel left, but not before he gave a polite nod in the direction of our car. This time I managed a friendly "Woof!"

Jesna had a tear in her eye. Then she turned to Pete and said, "Pete, by God's grace, and if you ask, you could have God's Son living in your heart. That's what it means to be 'born again.'"

FAMILY DISCUSSION

1. Why do you think Mary was so willing to take on the tough job of having and raising God's Son?

2. How does having God inside of you—being born again— cause you to act differently?

3. Have you been born again? Would you like to be born again? [Parents; pray with your children to receive Christ into their hearts. Lead them in this prayer: "Jesus, please come and live in my heart. Please show me what you want me to be."]

SCENE FOUR
MARY'S VISIT TO ELIZABETH[6]

Mary didn't even hesitate. Moments after Gabriel had evaporated into the early-morning air, she got to her feet and began to walk away from the small city.

We followed slowly behind her. I believe that every rock in the path left an imprint in my backside as we bounced our way up into the hill country of Judah. What these time machines had in speed, they lacked in shock absorption.

The sun had just pushed off from the horizon when Priscilla broke the silence. "OK, OK, I'll admit this is sorta fun. But Jesna, you said we would be back before 1:31 P.M., and we've been here for way longer than any sixty seconds."

Jesna smiled at Priscilla. "You haven't checked your watch lately, have you?"

"No," said Priscilla, glancing down to observe the small computer that was strapped to her wrist, "But I knooooooooooow," and she dragged that word out almost to the length of a sentence, "that it's been way more than any… uh… *What in the world! My watch has stopped!*"

"What does your watch say, Priscilla?"

"Nothing."

Pete interrupted. "That's right 'cause watches don't talk."

"Very funny garbage-disposal-boy, but my watch is broken, and that's not funny. I just put new batteries in it yesterday."

"But what does your watch say, Priscilla?" Jesna asked again as Mrs. Pilgrim took her turn applying a hand to Pete's mouth.

"It says exactly what it did when we got into this car, 1:30:01. And that was a long time ago."

"All that means, Priscilla, is that we have not been gone one earth-second, at least not yet. You have entered into the realm of 'the kingdom.' Time and space are not the same here. In fact, there is only one thing that is exactly the same in both places."

"What's that?" Pete asked, prying his mother's fingers off his mouth.

"Love," Jesna said. "It's the most powerful and persistent force in the universe."

"But, if we take this whole ride," Pete moaned, oblivious to the profound nature of Jesna's reply, "I might not get back until I'm an old man, like Dad."

"Hey, what do you mean?" said Dad as he reached out his hand toward Pete, but Pete ducked away.

"No," Jesna laughed, "we'll be back before one earth-minute has passed. Trust me."

I guess it's pretty hard not to trust someone with golden hair who looks only five years old. So, no one jumped out of the car. We kept following as that same young, Jewish girl with dusty feet made her way along narrow, dirt paths.

Finally, after more Bible-time passed than it would take me to catch a whole herd of cats, we arrived at civilization. We followed Mary through the narrow streets of a town that appeared to be carved right out of a hillside.

The streets were lined with people of all sizes and shapes and smells; and I don't believe a one of them had ever seen a razor. It seemed that most of the people were shouting, trying to sell stuff—bread, meat, cloth—to each other. Mary seemed undistracted.

"Hey!" shouted Pete, "We were just here. That's the building we crashed through."

He was right. In front of us was the very same temple where Gabriel had winked at me. "I still can't believe there isn't a big hole in the side of it," Pete said.

Mary turned a corner. In moments she was rapping on a rough-hewn wooden door. The door swung open and before you could blink, Mary was gobbled up by the hugs and kisses of an olive-skinned woman who had a bright face and dull grey hair.

"That's Elizabeth, Zachariah's wife," Jesna told us. "She's Mary's cousin."

Before she pulled Mary into her house and almost right out of her sandals, Elizabeth said some tender words I will never forget.

"Mary, when the sound of your 'Hello' first reached my ears, the baby that is in my womb leapt with joy, and I was filled with the joy of the Holy Spirit. You're so blessed among women, and the baby in your womb is also blessed! I just cannot imagine why I am so blessed that the mother of my Lord visits me!"

When Mary heard these words she dropped to her knees, as if her skeleton suddenly took a coffee break. And, as she and Elizabeth cried for joy together, we all heard Mary's voice when she lifted her head and said to Elizabeth:

"I'm bursting with God-news;
I'm dancing the song of my Savior God.
God took one good look at me, and look what happened—
I'm the most fortunate woman on earth!
What God has done for me will never be forgotten,
the God whose very name is holy, set apart from all others.
His mercy flows in wave after wave
on those who are in awe before him.
He bared his arm and showed his strength,...
He knocked tyrants off their high horses,
pulled victims out of the mud.
The starving poor sat down to a banquet;
the callous rich were left out in the cold.
He embraced his chosen child, Israel;
he remembered and piled on the mercies,
piled them high.
It's exactly what he promised,
beginning with Abraham and right up to now."[7]

For once the Pilgrims, including Pete, were speechless. But not Jesna, who quietly whispered, "Two babies, not yet out of their

mothers' wombs, have recognized each other and danced. Two
mothers-to-be: one old enough to be a grandmother, the other
young enough to play with dolls. But they both know that they
have been chosen to give birth to the future—God come down to
earth, wearing flesh like an overcoat, and his messenger."

Even Priscilla was crying. What she had just seen would have
been impossible for anyone to make up.

FAMILY DISCUSSION

1. Why do you think baby Jesus' cousin jumped while he was still
   inside his mother's womb?

2. Have you ever felt like jumping when you think about Jesus?

3. Tell us about it.

SCENE FIVE
THE BIRTH OF JOHN THE BAPTIST[8]

"Hold on to your stomachs," Jesna said in her
softest, smallest voice. Then, the strangest thing
happened. It was as if all of us were at the still,
calm, center of a storm of swirling flashes of lights
and colors.

Jesna explained, "We're just sitting tight for a bit while three
months of time passes by."

"Huh?" said the four Pilgrims. I whined.

If you've ever heard a song played at a real fast speed, then you
can imagine what we saw—sort of. Better yet, it was more like
watching all three of the Star Wars movies in about five seconds,

from inside the screen! It was wild! But when it stopped, we were once again staring at the front wall of Elizabeth's and Zachariah's house.

"Let's go in," Jesna suggested. We climbed out of our car, walked across tightly-packed sand that was as hard as concrete, toward the open front door.

"I've got to go to the bathroom," Pete said. "I haven't been in over three months, y'know."

"Actually Pete, as far as your stomach and those other matters are concerned, you've only been gone for a few seconds," Jesna reminded him again.

"I know; I was just kidding."

"Pete," Priscilla said as she gave her brother an elbow to the stomach, "don't kid like that. You don't see a McDonald's around here that we can just duck into, do you?"

"McDonald's! I could eat a McHorse!"

"Look!" said Jesna, "It's John, Jesus' cousin. The baby that will grow up to be called 'John the Baptist.'"

The room was packed with people. But there, in the center, the old priest Zachariah's face was beaming like a flashlight. He was holding a bundle of cloth close to his chest. His wife, Elizabeth, sat on a wooden stool beside him. Her face was bright enough to make you squint, too.

"What are you going to name the baby?" I heard someone call out.

"Don't ask him!" came a whispered voice from the crowd. "You know he hasn't been able to talk for more than nine months."

"Well, he can write, can't he?"

"He'll name him Zach, Jr., of course," another voice said.

"What else would a priest name his son?"

A chorus of "Oh, yeah's" followed.

Zachariah looked at his wife and nodded. She stood to her feet and spoke. "No, his name is John."

"But," someone in the crowd said, "no one in your family is named that."

"Yeah, why don't you just call him Herod, if you want to pick a stupid name?"

"Shhhh!" someone else said.

Then, Zachariah turned to Elizabeth and gently handed her the cooing bundle of cloth, as if it contained a quart jar of nitro-glycerin. He picked up what looked like a thin piece of cardboard from a wooden table and wrote on it with a stick, or something I could imagine fetching.

Then, he held up the finished product so that everyone in the room could read it. It looked like chicken-scratches to me, but I heard several people exclaim, "His name is John?"

Then everyone gasped as Zachariah grabbed his face with both hands and started moving his mouth as a fish might. They gasped even louder when he started talking—right out loud—and praising God! Even I could tell that God was present in that room, and I'm a dog.

In a deep rich voice Zachariah began to prophesy:

"Blessed be the Lord, the God of Israel;
he came and set his people free....
"And you, my child, 'Prophet of the Highest,'
will go ahead of the Master to prepare his ways,
Present the offer of salvation to his people,
the forgiveness of their sins.
"Through the heartfelt mercies of our God,
God's Sunrise will break in upon us,
Shining on those in the darkness,
those sitting in the shadow of death,
Then showing us the way, one foot at a time,
down the path of peace."⁹

When he finished there was a deep silence in the room. Mrs. Pilgrim was squeezing Pete's hand.

FAMILY DISCUSSION

1. How do you think Zachariah felt when he got his voice back?

2. Do you think it was difficult for Zachariah to go against the opinions of his friends and neighbors and do what God told him to do, naming his son John?

3. How does someone hear what God wants to tell him?

4. Have you ever heard God talking to you?

5. Consider taking a few minutes now, or sometime tomorrow, to be completely quiet. See if that helps you hear God's voice more clearly.

SCENE SIX
THE GENEALOGY OF JESUS[10]

 We all filed back to the car and took our seats. I snuggled down between Pete and Priscilla. Then, with a sudden flash of light and a head-snapping jerk we were off again. When our car came to a stop we were in what appeared to be a long, dark, oversized hallway. Actually it was more like a tunnel.

We sat silently, in the thick darkness. Then, just to our right, a large three-dimensional figure appeared. It was the image of a man, but bigger than life. He had long, flowing white hair, a white mustache, and a white beard to match. The beard went from his chin to about where a navel would be.

You could see the figure and you could also see right through it. It was like a hologram. Then, without warning, the image began to move and to speak. It said, in a very deep voice, "Shalom, Pilgrims. My name is Abraham.

"Over four thousand years ago my wife Sarah had the un-speakable joy of giving birth to our son. We named him Isaac, a name that means, 'one laughs'.

"It's true that he was a smiling, laughing baby. But now I know that it was a more appropriate name than either of us knew. He was God's first seedling in the kingdom of joy he was planting on earth."

Then suddenly Abraham was gone, and just as suddenly another appeared, this time to our left. "My name is Isaac," he said. "You've already heard from my dad. I grew up and married Rebeccah, and we were the proud parents of Esau and Jacob."

As soon as Isaac had spoken these words, Jacob appeared and

spoke to us. And then Judah, and Perez and, well, many, many others, with names like Amminadab, Boaz, Jesse, and David. He was wearing a purple robe and a crown on his head. Then there was Jehoshaphat and Uzziah, Hezekiah, and Josiah, and on and on, until one, with a very kind face and loving eyes, said: "My name is Joseph, I married Mary, and through a miracle of the Holy Spirit of God, we had a Son. I'm sure you all have heard of him. His name is Jesus. His real Father is also your own real Father."

Priscilla and Pete looked at their father with question marks in their eyes.

"His name is God."

Then, the images stopped appearing and Jesna spoke out of the darkness, "There were fourteen generations from Abraham to David, another fourteen from David to Jehoiachin and the sending away of Israel into Babylon, and yet another fourteen from the time of the Babylonian exile to the birth of Jesus, the Christ."

"Wow!" said Priscilla. "That's forty-two generations, or six times seven generations. And, they were divided into three groups of the exact same size—Abraham to David, David to Babylon, and Babylon to Jesus. Do you know the odds of something like that happening by chance?"

"Yes," said Jesna, as Priscilla was poking away at her wrist computer. "There is a smaller than tiny chance something like that could happen without someone to plan it; and, there's a very, very large chance that it was put together by a loving God, who writes lessons into history using the lives of his people as his ink and paper."

"Yep!" said Priscilla, as she stared at the hardware on her wrist. "That's exactly right."

FAMILY DISCUSSION

1. The births of John and Jesus were part of a great plan God had. It was all part of a big design. Have you ever thought about the fact that you, too, were created to fit into this design?

2. How does it feel to know that your creation was by design?

3. God's word says that when we become Christians, we are made part of his family tree. What's the importance of being part of the family of God?

SCENE SEVEN
THE BIRTH OF JESUS[11]

In an instant we were airborne. While our car was still a car, it was rapidly gaining altitude. If the hallway we were in had a top to it, it was nowhere to be found.

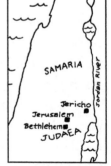

Gradually, the darkness above us was pricked by pinpoints of light that slowly became a night sky. The darkness below us also began to glow—from the lights of dozens of towns and villages.

"Look," Jesna said. "See that big patch of light there?" And we quickly saw a large square with flickering lights of fires and torches everywhere. It looked like a star sleeping on the ground. "That's the city of Jerusalem. Isn't it gorgeous?"

No one answered Jesna. They were all too busy holding on to the sides of the car. Even in the darkness I could see four sets of white knuckles and I was digging my toenails into the seat.

"Now," said Jesna, "look over there. That's where we will be landing—that little town just a few miles to the southwest of Jerusalem. It's called Bethlehem."

Jesna continued talking to us, her captive audience, as our car began to descend through the cool night air. "The name Bethlehem means 'house of bread', but most people refer to it as 'the city of David', after King David."

"Jesna," Pete managed, "why are there so many people on the road tonight? Is there a war or something going on?"

"No, Pete, there's not a war going on. Caesar Augustus (uh, he's sort of like the President, if the whole world had a president) has ordered that all of the people in his Empire be counted, as part of a census. All the people heading to Bethlehem are descendants of King David. They have to go back to their own ancestral hometown to be counted."

Just then our car came to a bumpy stop on the ground. "Look," Jesna said in a whisper.

We looked and saw a pile of wood and straw that resembled the remains of a barn, half eaten by time. "Let's go inside," Jesna said.

"I don't believe that place has an inside," said Pete, as he climbed out of the car. "It looks like it's all outside."

We all tiptoed behind Jesna as she quietly walked through the opening of the barn. Then we sat down on some straw, still in single file.

"Hey!" Pete said in a loud whisper. "That's the same girl we saw at Zach and Elizabeth's house. Ain't it?"

"Isn't she," Mrs. Pilgrim corrected.

"That's what *I'm* asking!" Pete chirped.

"Yeah," Priscilla followed. "It is and that man is the last one we saw back in the hallway."

"That's right," Jesna said, in a voice that was more reverent than you would expect to hear in church. "That's Mary and Joseph. And that," she said as Mary lifted a bundle of cloth from the container where donkeys eat, "is the King of all kings, the very Son of the Creator of the Universe."

"Get outa here," Pete groaned out, "It's a little homeless baby whose parents are so poor that he had to be born out here in the middle of all this straw and manure. I mean, I might have been born at night, but it wasn't last night. If God was going to send his baby to earth, I bet he would have sent it to that Caesar Septemberus' house."

"That's Caesar Augustus," Priscilla said as her elbow pushed into Pete's ribs.

"Ouch!"

"No," Jesna said to Pete, "I can see that there's much for you to learn about your other father. But, we'll start with this.

"God is filled with so much love for all his children that he sent his own infant Son into their world to save them from the Prince of Darkness. And, he wanted the Savior to be *with* his children, not *above*, or *over* them. He wanted him to be with them in the straw, the dirt, the pain, and the manure.

"And, he certainly wanted the One who will be the sustainer of their new life—the 'Bread' of their new life—to be born in a place called, 'The House of Bread.' God has always found it hard to resist a good object lesson."

We all thought about what Jesna had said for a long moment, until the baby in the cow feeder called for our attention. Baby Jesus was stirring in his sleep.

FAMILY DISCUSSION

1. Why do you think the Creator of the universe chose to be born in a barn?
2. What do you think it felt like to go from being King of everything to being a helpless and poor baby, as Jesus did?
3. How would it change the way you act to know that the King of the universe is going to be with you in a sad or lonely place?

SCENE EIGHT
THE ADORATION OF THE INFANT JESUS[12]

"Come on," Jesna said as she stood to her feet. "There's something you've got to see."

"But, can't we just stay here a little longer?" Pete asked.

"We'll be right back," Jesna reassured.

We all followed Jesna back out to the car, climbed in, and, in an instant, we were off again. This time the car ascended straight up, like a helicopter, toward the stars. For the second time in less than ten Bethlehem-minutes we could see the little town's lights flickering below.

We glided slowly and silently through the air, which smelled of burning wood and roasted meat, until the lights below disappeared into a quilt of darkness.

Then we began to descend into the dark, eventually coming back to earth a few feet from a short, old tree whose branches looked like the tangle a cat might make with a ball of yarn.

Immediately, we heard voices. Looking out we saw a group of men and boys huddled around the embers of a fire. "Phew-wee,"

Pete said, "What is that awful smell?"

"Shhhh!" Mr. Pilgrim spoke forcefully in Pete's direction. "They might hear you."

"That's OK," said Jesna, "No one but the angels and the animals can see us. Those men are shepherds and, it *is* a pretty bad smell to be downwind of."

"Well, I wish we couldn't smell them," Pete moaned.

Jesna giggled as she said, "They don't get much chance, out here, to take hot baths. You'll get used to it. The sheep do."

Just then, the angel Gabriel was back. He stood with them, lighting up their faces and the countryside like a giant torch.

The shepherds cowered in fear, just like we had the first time we saw him. Gabriel spoke:

"Don't be afraid. I'm here to announce a great and joyful event that is meant for everybody, worldwide: a Savior has just been born in David's town...."

"I know," Pete said in an excited whisper. "We just saw him, didn't we?"

"… a Savior who is Messiah and Master. This is what you're to look for: a baby wrapped in a blanket and lying in a manger."

"In a manger?" one of the shepherds managed to mumble. But, before the question mark was placed at the end of his sentence, the sky exploded. Gabriel was joined by a huge diamond-shaped choir of angels, and they were singing:

"Glory to God in the heavenly heights,
Peace to all men and women on earth who please him."[13]

In a little while the singing angels and Gabriel faded into the night air like thinning vapor, leaving only the stars and dying fire for light.

"Let's get over to Bethlehem as fast as we can and see for ourselves what God wants to show us," one of the shepherds said.

"Aren't they going to take a bath first?"

"Hush, Pete."

We followed along behind the jogging band of sheep-keepers as they made their way to Bethlehem.

Even though they had heard Gabriel say they would find Jesus in a manger, they were unable to resist the temptation to stop and inquire at several of the nicer hotels in town.

Each time they were met by angry voices and hands that waved them on. It was hard to resist the temptation to jump down from the car and lead them to the old barn, like Lassie might do.

Eventfully they found their way to the open doorway of the

world's first and most spectacular church. They entered and saw Mary and Joseph, eyes still locked in a loving gaze upon God's little boy.

The shepherds dropped to their knees in hushed awe. Time stood still. The noise of distant crowds and howling dogs never seemed so out of place, or so unimportant.

Eventually, Mary and Joseph turned their attention to their guests. In excited whispers, the shepherds told them what they had seen. Mary smiled a knowing smile. And then the shepherds left—but often returned to gaze at God's special star.

Some time later, when Joseph and Mary had moved to a house, more visitors came to see them—three men wearing bright silk and funny hats.

Like the shepherds, these men fell to their knees when they saw the young child. What a sight! Mary and Joseph—the standing poor. The kneeling rich Kings. A laughing baby-God.

"How did you know to come here?" Mary asked the three.

"We are scholars," the oldest said. "We have spent our lives searching for truth and wisdom. In the book of your own prophet, Micah, he wrote plainly for all to read:

It's you, Bethlehem, in Judah's land,
no longer bringing up the rear.
From you will come the leader
who will shepherd-rule my people, my Israel."[14]

"Hum, 'shepherd-rule', I like that!" said one of the sheep-keepers who had returned for another peek at God.

"Me too," Jesna whispered.

FAMILY DISCUSSION

1. Why do you think that God arranged for shepherds to be the first to visit his son?

2. How do you think the shepherds felt when they saw baby Jesus?

3. Do you think their lives will be different because of the moments they shared with Jesus in the barn? In what ways?

SCENE NINE
THE CIRCUMCISION[15]

The beauty and charm of the infant was so great that we could not bear to leave him.

It only took a few "Puleeeezzes" from Pete and a yelp or two from me to convince Jesna to let us stay a while longer—instead of getting back into the time machine.

The "while" turned into eight days. But, since that amount of time passed before Priscilla's watch could tick, even once, no one in the Pilgrim family became hungry or thirsty-not even Pete.

When the baby was awake, we all stood around him, gazing and smiling. Priscilla quickly became convinced that he could see us, even though Mary and Joseph couldn't. Jesna said she was right.

I'm pretty sure I saw him smile, right at me, once. And, when a loud "Moo" from the cow called everyone's attention away, I licked him, from chin to forehead.

When the baby slept, we played with the animals (they could definitely see and hear us) and went on short tours of the little town of Bethlehem. We never went far, though. We didn't want to miss one waking moment with the baby.

Once, I heard Mrs. Pilgrim ask Mr. Pilgrim if he wanted to have another baby. He was quiet for a long time before saying, "Nah, babies like this one don't come along very often."

"About once in history," Jesna offered.

On the morning of the eighth day, Joseph was looking a little queasy, and a whole lot nervous. After a while, he and Mary began to search through the bundles which were their belongings.

Their search ended and they spread a white cloth across one of the few piles of hay the cow and donkey had not yet eaten. On the cloth Joseph placed a piece of flint which had real sharp edges, like a knife. His hands were trembling, just like my paws did once when I was hiding from a pit bull.

"Hey! What's going on here?" Priscilla asked Jesna.

Jesna placed her small five-year-old hand on one of Priscilla's clenched fists. "This is a very special time in the life of a Jewish family. After a baby boy is eight days old, the father makes a mark on the baby to show that the little boy really belongs to another Daddy—God. It's the sign of a promise made between God and Abraham, over 2,000 years ago."

"Yea," said Pete, "but that looks like a knife Joseph has in his hand. And..." he said in an increasingly shrill voice, "he's walking over to where the baby is."

"That's right, Pete."

"He's not gonna do it!" Pete said as he jumped to his feet and began searching the ground for a rock. "I'll knock Joseph upside the head first." And with that, Pete reached down, grabbed a rock from the stable floor.

"No!" Pete's mother screamed.

"Sit down. Now!" his father said in a very firm voice.

"But Dad," Priscilla pleaded, "he is going to cut the baby. Jesna even said so."

"That's none of our business. You heard her say the Jewish people have been doing this for 2,000 years. What's happening here is called 'the covenant of circumcision.' It's part of being a Jewish baby boy—a way of showing that you belong to God."

Just then their conversation was interrupted by something they didn't want to hear. The baby was crying.

"See! I told you he was going to hurt him." And just as Pete let go of his last word, he also let go of the rock. It sailed, unnoticed, over the head of Joseph.

"Pete!" shouted both of the Pilgrim parents.

"It's OK, Pete," Jesna said in a soft voice as she placed her hand on Pete's. "It's OK that you are angry. And, it's OK that the baby is crying. I'll bet even his other Father, God, winced a little bit.

"You see, Pete, that baby over there is more special than you can imagine. He's God's very own, very dear Son, come to earth as a baby to help people find the way back to their real homes, with God.

"But to do it, Pete, he had to become just like us, in a human body. It's sort of like if Wisdom got lost and because you love her so much you were willing to become a dog, just like her, so you could sniff her out, and in dog language, tell her how to get back.

But, it's even more special than that. That little baby has also agreed to feel all the pain that humans feel, and to cry salty tears, just like they do. This won't be the last time he'll be cut, and bleed."

Jesna was interrupted by the deep voice of Joseph, who spoke loudly, as if there were hundreds of people in the barn. "His name will be 'Jesus.'"

Mary held the baby and cried along with baby Jesus.

FAMILY DISCUSSION

1. The mark on the baby was to show he belonged to God. What shows you belong to God?

2. God expects us to cut away—give up—certain things when we give our hearts to God. What kinds of things should we stop doing?

SCENE TEN
THE FLIGHT INTO EGYPT[16]

"Back in the car now," Jesna said, firmly. We all backed out of the barn, eyes glued to baby Jesus, feeling our way to the car with the heels of our feet.

When we had settled into our seats, the car began to move. We rode over a dusty, five-mile stretch of path, which wound its way toward Jerusalem.

As we traveled, Pete said, "I think when the angels were putting rocks all over the earth, one of them must have tripped and spilled a bag right here." I think he was right.

The path became a road, and we followed it up to the walls that surrounded Jerusalem, and then through a huge archway made from carved stones. We continued over narrow streets, crowded with merchants, wonderful smells, and the laughter of children.

We didn't stop until we had driven up and across a large stone porch and right through the wall of another temple. We were so used to driving through stone that no one even ducked this time. Although, Pete did manage to let out a "Cool!"

We were inside a room that Jesna said was called "the Holy Place." It was about as long as eight elephants standing in a straight line, trunk-to-tail, and about half that wide. It was as high as four basketball goals, all stacked on top of each other.

"Where does that door go to?" Pete asked Jesna, in a whisper.

"It goes into the 'Holy of Holies.' Only priests can go into that room; and even they aren't allowed to enter very often."

"Hum," Pete said, with a mischievous ring in his voice. "Let's go in there!"

"No!" everyone said at once.

Then Jesna reached down to the dash of the car and pressed a button. Just as had happened in front of Zach and Elizabeth's house, things began to move around us very, very fast—like you were watching a whole video movie in just a few seconds, from the inside.

She pressed the button again and the world around us again played at normal speed.

"Look!" said Priscilla. She was pointing to what looked like an altar, in front of the door to the Holy of Holies. "It's Mary and Joseph."

"That's right." Jesna began to explain. "They have come to the Temple in Jerusalem to offer baby Jesus back to God."

"You mean they aren't going to be his parents anymore? They're going to leave him here with that old man!" Pete's face was the picture of unbelief.

"No, Pete, it's just a special ceremony, a way of saying 'thank you' to God for giving them a baby to raise. It's a way of saying they know that all life really belongs to God, the Creator."

"Do you think that old priest guy knows who that Baby is? Do you want me to tell him?"

"Well," said Jesna, "if he doesn't, he's about to. Here comes Simeon."

Just then an old man wearing ragged clothes entered the temple, walked to where the ceremony was going on, and took baby Jesus into his arms. He began to speak, like he was preaching:

"God, you can now release your servant;
release me in peace as you promised.
With my own eyes I've seen your salvation;
it's now out in the open for everyone to see:
A God-revealing light to the not-Jewish nations,
and of glory for your people Israel."[17]

The force of the man's words froze Pete in his tracks. Mary began to cry. The tears sparkled on her glowing face like two rivers on the moon.

Joseph's eyes were closed; he was praying. The priest just stood there with his mouth sprung open.

"Look at the priest," Pete said. "I bet I could shoot a basketball right into his mouth."

"He's just surprised, Pete," Jesna said. "He probably wasn't expecting a Baby-Messiah to come by this morning."

Then, an older lady, Anna, who was almost a hundred years old, walked over to the altar. She burst out talking really loudly about who Baby Jesus was to everyone in the Temple.

When the service—and all the unexpected sermons—were over, Mary, who was holding Jesus, and Joseph turned and began to walk out. When they got right in front of us they stopped, and Joseph began to whisper to Mary.

He told her that last night he had a dream. He said that Gabriel had appeared to him and told him, "You must take the Child and his mother to Egypt. Stay there until further notice. King Herod is on the hunt for this Child, and wants to kill him."

He told Mary he thought they should leave for Egypt at once. Mary nodded, and they left.

"So," said Pete, "Are we going to Egypt now?"

"No," Jesna answered. "We'll let them take that trip alone. We'll catch up with them after they get back to their home town of Nazareth. By then Jesus will be a twelve-year-old young man."

FAMILY DISCUSSION

1. What do you think it meant for Mary and Joseph to offer their baby back to God?

2. How do you think the priest felt when he heard the two prophecies about baby Jesus being the long-awaited Messiah?

3. What differences does it make in our lives—in the holy place in our heart—when we recognize Jesus as the Messiah?

SCENE ELEVEN
THE CHILDHOOD OF JESUS[18]

"But, but, I want to go with them to Egypt. I want to see him grow up," Pete stammered, his eyes pleading with Jesna.

"I'm sorry Pete, but the Bible doesn't tell us much about the boyhood of Jesus. I wish it did. This is a ride through the pages of the Gospels, so, this car only takes us on tours through words that are recorded in the Bible."

"Bummer!"

"I'd be glad to tell you what I know about those years, Pete." Pete's nodding head let Jesna know that he was interested. In fact, all the Pilgrims leaned forward to hear.

"Joseph and Mary headed southwest, to Egypt. Everything they owned was strapped to the back of their donkey. I don't think they even stopped back at the stable to pick up any of their things.

"I don't know how they supported themselves in Egypt. Maybe God used ravens to send them food, like he had done with Elijah. Maybe Joseph worked as a carpenter—that's what he had been doing in Nazareth."

"Or," Pete interrupted, "maybe Mary sold Tupperware to the Egyptians."

At that Priscilla's eyes rolled up in her head in a "can you believe it?" look.

"Maybe, Pete. But all that is really known is that they lived in Egypt under God's watchful eye. After they had been there for a time, Joseph had another dream."

"Boy," said Pete, "he sure dreams a lot. I dream a lot too, when I've had pizza. Do you think…"

"No, Pete, there was no pizza back then. God was using Joseph's dreams as a way to talk with him. Anyway, God told Joseph that it was time to go back to Bethlehem. They packed up and left. On the way back, they learned that the king's brother was ruling over that area. Perhaps, because of this, they were afraid to go back there. Instead they went to Galilee, and lived in a town called Nazareth."

"That's where they were from to start with," Priscilla announced.

"Yes, they ended up going back home to live. And in his parents' hometown, Jesus grew strong in body, wise in mind, and humble in spirit. The grace of his Father, God, was on him."

"I bet he was great at Nintendo games, being God and everything."

"They didn't have Nintendo games then, Pete, and, although he was completely God, he was also completely man."

"Sorta like Superman in Clark Kent's clothes?"

"Ummm, not exactly. More like you, with Superman buried deep, deep down inside."

"I like that!" Pete said, as a wide grin spread out over his face.

"But Jesna," Priscilla interrupted, "Why did they have to go to Egypt? It seems like such a waste of their time."

"I don't know, Priscilla. But, do you remember in the Old Testament when Joseph was taken to Egypt and later was able to save the lives of his family?"

"Yes."

"Me too," said Pete.

"And do you remember that four hundred years later Moses led the Israelites out of Egypt to live in the Promised Land?"

"Yes."

"Yep."

"Well, maybe God wanted to show the world that a different Joseph (the father of Jesus on earth) was on the scene, and that a new and better Moses (Baby Jesus) would lead his people (those who truly believed he was God's Son), out of Egypt. In the Bible, Egypt always stands for a place of sin. Jesus was going to lead them into a new and better Promised Land, which is the Kingdom of God."

"There surely are lots of homecomings in the Bible," Mrs. Pilgrim said.

"Yes," Jesna continued. "And you'll see later that he even provides a new and improved 'manna.' Himself. He is the Bread of Life."

FAMILY DISCUSSION

1. What do you think Jesus was like as a boy?

2. What do you think it felt like for Mary and Joseph to watch the Son of God growing up before their eyes?

3. If you were going to live like Jesus did when he was a boy, what might you do?

SCENE TWELVE
THE BOY JESUS IN THE TEMPLE[19]

Jesna pushed the button again, the one that made the world around us play on superfast speed. Only this time, the world whizzed past even faster.

As we sat very still and quiet in the car, a typhoon of streaking colors blew all around us. Then the flying colors stopped, and we saw that we were still sitting inside the Temple, in Jerusalem.

The Temple was *packed* with people and contained all the noise of a Notre Dame football stadium on homecoming day.

"The year," Jesna said, in her five-year-old-tour-guide voice, "is approximately A.D. 12."

"Give or take four years for calendar accuracy," Priscilla chimed in. Jesna looked impressed.

"Wow," Pete exclaimed, "A.D. 12. If I find some old money around here, will it have B.C. printed on it?"

"No, dummy," Priscilla snapped, "How would the money-makers know when Jesus was going to be born?"

"Those wiseguys we saw in Bethlehem said it was in the book! Didn't they?"

Jesna continued as if no one had spoken. "The baby Jesus has become a boy of twelve years.

"The Temple, its outer court, and the whole city of Jerusalem are full of people because one of the seven special feasts that the Jewish people celebrate has just come to an end. It was the week-long celebration of Passover.

"Sometimes they call it the 'Feast of Unleavened Bread,' because they first started celebrating it back before Moses was given the Ten Commandments, to rejoice about their escape from Egypt to the Promised Land. When they escaped, there wasn't time for the bread to rise."

"I didn't know bread did that," Pete said. "What if it rises so much it pops out of its plastic wrapper?"

Jesna continued while shaking her head and staring at Pete. "As I was saying. These people in the temple today don't know that a whole new exodus or escape is now possible for them. Or soon will be."

"You're talking about Jesus aren't you?" Pete asked.

"Yes, that's right."

"Well, where is he? I'd really like to see him again. He'd be in the sixth grade now, you know, just like Prissy was last year."

"He's right over there, Pete."

We looked in the direction where Jesna was pointing with one of her tiny fingers. Through the milling crowd we saw a circle of men, mostly old men, dressed in black robes, their faces thick with fur, some sitting, some standing, surrounding a young boy.

We could only see glimpses of the boy through the crowd of men standing around him.

He was wearing a light-colored robe. His hair was a sea of dark brown waves. His face was bright, youthful, and still grew only peach fuzz. It was a strange sight—a young boy holding a score of adults captive with his words.

"Jesus! Jesus!" The circle of men was split in two by a young woman who ran to Jesus.

We moved closer in our car. We could see that the woman's face showed anger and joy, dismay and relief. It was busier than a flashing neon sign.

"Jesus! We have been worried sick about you. Joseph and I thought you were walking with your cousins. I thought I would die when I realized you weren't with them."

"I'm sorry, Mother," Jesus said as he hugged his mother tightly. Then he said:

"Why were you looking for me? Didn't you know that I had to be here, dealing with the things of my Father?"[20]

From the puzzled looks on the faces of Mary and Joseph, it was very clear that they did not know.

Mary reached out and gave Jesus a tender touch on the cheek. I think she just wanted to see if he was still made of flesh.

FAMILY DISCUSSION

1. What do you think it would feel like to have a room full of adults sit down and listen to what you have to say?

2. What do you think Jesus was talking about—to the adults in the Temple?

3. Do you think Jesus might talk to you, if you would stop to listen?

SCENE THIRTEEN
JOHN THE BAPTIST[21]

In an instant we exploded through a kaleidoscope of lights and bright, swirling colors. Jesna explained, "Eighteen years are reeling past us. The next time you see Jesus he will be a grown man, thirty years old."

As soon as her last word was spoken, we exited the colorful time tunnel. Below us was desert sand and rocks. Above us was a cloudless, blue canopy. Around us were hundreds of people, dressed in bathrobes, staring straight ahead.

Words echoed in our ears like thunder: "Change the way you are living your life. God's kingdom is here, and you are invited to live in it. Prepare for God's arrival! Make the road to his kingdom smooth and straight!"

Twenty yards in front of us we could see the man from whose mouth the storm of words had blown. He was standing thigh-deep in river water. He looked to be about thirty sun-hardened years old; and he was wearing what appeared to be the remains of a camel after a pack of lions had finished with it. His hairy shirt was tied around his waist by a thin strip of leather.

"Is that Jesus?" Pete asked. "Man, has he *changed!*"

"No Pete," Jesna said. "That's not Jesus. That's his cousin John."

"John the Methodist? Elizabeth and Zachariah's son?"

"Uh, not exactly, Pete. He's John the Baptist. He's called 'baptist' because he baptizes people, plunges them in water to show everyone that they are clean from their sins and ready to enter God's kingdom. Look, he's about to baptize someone now."

We looked. John had grabbed someone by the back and the

face and he pushed them, face over back, into the river.

"Is he going to kill 'em Dad?"

"Shhhhh!"

"In a manner of speaking," Jesna inserted.

Then John pulled the man up out of the water. The wet man hugged John, turned, and walked out of the water with his hands over his head, talking to the blue sky, his face all smiles.

"What's he so happy about?" Priscilla asked, with a frown on her face. "It's going to take a long time for that bathrobe to dry. He'll probably get a rash."

"He's happy, Priscilla, because all of his sins are gone just like sticks floating downstream; and because he knows he's been invited to live life a whole different way—as a subject in God's kingdom. He's ready to hear and understand the teachings of Jesus."

"Well what gives Cousin John the right to tell people they can go and live in God's kingdom?" Priscilla continued.

"Several things, Priscilla. He's of priestly descent—on both his father's and his mother's sides of the family. Remember, you saw his dad's line in the temple, and his mom's line goes all the way back to the first priest, Aaron. He's spent his entire life preparing for this special job of introducing Jesus to everyone who will listen. And, as you remember, he was filled by the Holy Spirit while he was still in his mother's body."

"Oh," Priscilla said, and you could see she was thinking hard.

FAMILY DISCUSSION

1. Why do you think that John the Baptist wasn't very concerned about his appearance?

2. Why do you think the "baptized" people were acting so happy?

3. How do you think you might have acted if you had been baptized by John?

SCENE FOURTEEN
JOHN'S PREACHING OF REPENTANCE[22]

As we continued to watch we saw that there was a long line of people, waiting to have John baptize them. The line went from the riverbank, back and forth, up and over the sand and rocks, like a blast from a can of Pete's Silly String.

"I don't understand this," Pete announced to no one in particular.

Most of the people in the back of the line looked pretty serious, like their taxes were being audited or something. They were dry-eyed and stared straight ahead.

Toward the middle of the line, most of the people had moist eyes, some had tears sliding down their faces, and quivering lips.

But before they got to John, most of the people had begun to cry really hard—many dropped to their knees, as if the weight of their tears was too much for their feet alone.

However, when John pulled them from the river, everything was changed. Most were beaming like Pete on Christmas morning. The ones who had seemed the saddest were now the most joyful.

I kept saying "most" because a few responded very differently, like they weren't even on the same path, the path that led from deep reflection, down through tears and anguish, to Christmas joy.

These few—most of them dressed in long black robes and wore high black hats and low gloomy faces—never shed a tear and never erupted with joy. This group just walked up to John, got wet, dripped river water, and walked away. From their expressions, they could just as easily have been in a line to have their mufflers repaired—assuming donkeys need replacements.

Evidently, Jesna noticed the same thing. She said, "See the ones dressed in black? They're called Pharisees. They probably aren't real serious about what is happening here, probably just showing up because it has become a popular thing to do."

Apparently John had noticed it too, and there wasn't a *probably* tone in his voice. After pulling yet another black-robed, tight-faced, Christmas-less Pharisee from the water, he spun around, faced the crowed and boomed out:

> "Brood of snakes! What do you think you're doing slithering down here to the river? Do you think a little water on your snakeskins is going to deflect God's judgment? It's your *life* that must change, not your skin. And don't think you can pull rank by claiming Abraham as 'father.' Being a child of Abraham is neither here nor there—children of Abraham are a dime a dozen.... What counts is your life. Is it green and blossoming? Because if it's deadwood, it goes on the fire."[23]

"Jesna," Priscilla asked, "Why is he so mad at them? At least they showed up. They could be out belching beer and betting on the camels."

Mr. and Mrs. Pilgrim looked at their daughter as if she were a Martian. Jesna just laughed. "That's a very good question, Priscilla. But I think I know the answer. Pharisees—and we'll be hearing from them quite a bit—have a real serious problem. They think they are already living in the 'kingdom' that Jesus has come to establish. But they are not."

"Then where do they live?" Pete asked.

"Well," Jesna answered, "I guess you could say they live in houses of straw and sticks."

"Like the first two little pigs," Pete interrupted.

"Sort of."

"And," Pete continued, "John is afraid that the big, bad, wolf will eat them."

"John knows that the big, bad, wolf helped them build their houses, and that they will never run to the safety of the real 'kingdom' so long as they believe that they are safe where they are now."

"No wonder John yelled so loud," Priscilla said. "They need to wake up and smell the manna."

"And speaking of manna," said Mr. Pilgrim, "look at this. 'Pharisee' comes right after 'pharaoh' in my pocket dictionary, and both the Pharisees and pharaoh were oppressors. They kept God's people in terrible bondage."

FAMILY DISCUSSION

1. When a baby is born it comes out of a sac of water in its mother's womb into the air of our world. How would you compare being born the first time and the baptizing John was doing?

2. If you had lived in the time of John the Baptist, would you have gotten in line to be baptized?

3. When you are born into your brand new life as a Christian, what are some of the first things you want to do?

SCENE FIFTEEN
JOHN REPLIES TO QUESTIONS[24]

It had been a few seconds since John had preached his brief sermon to the Pharisees; but the sound of his words was still rumbling through the valley, like a departing train. The crowd had become stone silent, mouths agape.

"Whoooeee!" said Pete, "John sure laid a guilt trip on everyone. They all look like they're in a movie, and the projector got stuck. Just look at their mouths hanging open."

"No, Pete, that's not it. John just told all the Pharisees that they aren't good enough to get into God's kingdom. Everybody in Israel thinks that no one can be any more righteous than the Pharisees. So, they're all stunned."

Then someone in the crowed blurted out, "Then what are we supposed to do?"

"Ah!" Pete said. "Somebody finally fixed the projector."

John answered, "If you have two coats, give one away. Do the same with your food."[25]

"So you have to be willing to be cold and hungry to get into the kingdom," Pete said. "I think I'll just stay outside with the serfs."

"No, Pete, he's not saying you have to be cold or hungry. But you do have to care so much for your friends, neighbors, and any other human being, that you would be willing to give them your *extra* coat or food. And that would leave both of you feeling very warm and satisfied."

Then someone else in the crowd, someone dressed in shiny silk, and wearing more gold than a professional football player, said, "Teacher, what should I do?"

"You should stop being an extortionist—collect only what is required by Roman law, and stop filling your pockets with other people's money."

"Is that man a politician, Dad? You said they are all crooks."

Mr. Pilgrim's face turned the color of my bright red dogfood dish.

Jesna answered Pete before the mercury in Mr. Pilgrim's thermometer blew out the top of his head. "That man is a tax collector. Sometimes the tax collectors took more money from the people than the law required and kept it for themselves. John is saying that in the kingdom, where you love your neighbor as yourself, you wouldn't think about cheating them. It would be like cheating yourself."

"Or like hitting yourself in the nose real hard?"

"Exactly, Pete."

Then a man dressed in a metal skirt and wearing a metal shirt stepped forward. He had a long spear in his right hand that he was using as a cane. "And what should we do?"

"You, soldier? No more shakedowns, no blackmail—and be content with your rations."

"Even the chopped camel on toast?" Pete giggled.

"Yes," Priscilla said in a deep voice, "even broccoli—without cheese." Pete gasped.

The soldier shook his head from side to side as he stepped back into the crowd.

Priscilla spoke up, "I don't get it. It sounds like John is saying that you have to be miserable to be happy. Is that it? These people just aren't miserable enough?"

"No, Priscilla. He's saying that you have to lose *yourself* and find love to be happy. It means putting down misery, not picking it up.

"The Pharisees," she continued, "are experts in SELF managed righteousness. They want to be in control, to make all the rules. John is telling the people that they need to become experts in GOD-managed righteousness, where God is in control and making the rules. And, God, you know, makes rules because he loves us."

FAMILY DISCUSSION

1. Why do you think John the Baptist did not like the religion of the Pharisees?

2. Why do people need to become experts in letting God be in control and make the rules?

3. If you gave God the reins of your life and let him run your life, how would things be different?

SCENE SIXTEEN
JOHN'S MESSIANIC PREACHING[26]

A murmur began in the crowd. It quickly spread and grew in volume until it sounded as if the people had become a volcano about to erupt. And then, they did.

"Are you the Christ, the Messiah?" an old man shouted above the noise. Before John could answer, a river of questions poured down the mountainside.

"Yeah, are you the One?"

"Are you the One the prophets have written about?"

"The One we have been waiting for since Moses?"

"Since Abraham?"

"Since Eden?"

"Are you the Messiah?"

"I AM NOT THE ONE!" John's thundering voice boomed out and turned their flood of questions off. He continued:

> "I'm baptizing you here in the river, turning your old life in for a kingdom life. The real action comes next: The main character in this drama—compared to him I'm a mere stagehand—will ignite the kingdom life within you, a fire within you, the Holy Spirit within you, changing you from the inside out. He's going to clean house—make a clean sweep of your lives. He'll place everything true in its proper place before God; everything false he'll put out with the trash to be burned."[27]

The crowd was stone silent. The Pilgrims were pebble silent. Jesna sat facing them, searching each of their faces. Words finally came—out of Mr. Pilgrim's mouth.

"Help us out here, Jesna. I don't get it. What is all this about having your insides burned up?"

"Yeah, and put out with the cat," Pete quickly added.

"The trash, Pete, put out with the trash, not the cat," Priscilla said. "He didn't say anything about a cat."

And Priscilla was right about that. Any self-respecting dog would have remembered it if he'd mentioned anything about cats. I would have remembered.

Jesna ignored Pete and Priscilla. "Well, Mr. Pilgrim, this is what I think. John is saying that he has a role to play in getting people ready to live a whole, new way as children in God's kingdom. His part in the world's greatest and longest running play is a small one, a bit part. Jesus will be the star.

"John's job is to preach to the people about their sins—the

ways they have learned to live under their own rule, instead of the rules of the 'King.'

"He hopes they will feel truly sorry, so sorry that they will come down to the river and be baptized, showing everyone they want to be forgiven, washed clean, and to live a whole new way. But that's all John can do for them. While they may leave the water more humble than when they entered it, they still have the same insides they had before their outsides got wet.

"To be really clean they will need another baptism. Their insides will need to be held under water, too, the water of the Holy Spirit of God. They need to be held under so long that everything that is false will drown in a river of Divine love.

"It's after baptism that true life begins. It's after baptism they truly become what Adam and Eve were before the fall—carefree children in their Father's kingdom. And the one who can do that, 'the Main Character,' is already standing in this crowd."

"Jesus!" said Mr. Pilgrim.

"Right, Dad," said Pete.

FAMILY DISCUSSION

1. If you had been listening to John, how do you think you might have felt?

2. How was a truly repentant person, who had been baptized by John, different from a baptized Pharisee?

3. How clean is your heart house? What will you do to make it ready for Jesus?

SCENE SEVENTEEN
THE BAPTISM OF JESUS[28]

"Look!" Jesna shouted. And look we did, like five chickens with spring-loaded heads. Jesna rarely got excited. If she hollered "Look!" there was, undoubtedly, something very special to see.

"Where? Where?" cried Pete. His head whipped back and forth as if he were watching a Ping-Pong tournament.

Priscilla was watching John. He stood, strangely silent, gazing right through the crowd. It seemed unusual for John not to be preaching and pointing, but I didn't think that was enough to make Jesna shout. It wasn't.

"There.... Up there.... Walking down the hillside." Jesna said this as she stood transfixed, pointing a tiny finger into the bathrobe-wearing crowd. She reminded me, for a moment, of my best friend. He's a bird dog.

As one, the crowd observed John's unearthly gaze. As one, they followed the path of his vision to a man who was on his way down the hill. Then the crowd slowly split in two. The man walked through the opening that had been created for him.

"That's Jesus," Jesna said in quiet, reverent voice. "That's Jesus."

I believe we were witnessing his first miracle. A throng of a thousand people had become so still and silent that you could hear the sand grinding under his sandals, as if he were walking on broken light bulbs.

Jesus was now thirty years old. He was ruggedly handsome (for a person), and he looked a lot like a picture I had seen of him in the house of one of Pete's friends. His hair was dark brown. It wasn't parted in the middle, like in the picture I saw. It was parted by the wind. A beard covered the lower portion of his face.

As he approached our car, I could see his eyes. They were brown windows to insides of tenderness and compassion. On the outside, however, he was an outdoorsman. And, after he passed us, the smell of freshly cut wood followed behind.

I later learned from Jesna that he had retired, just that day, from his job as a carpenter. "He decided to start working on human buildings" is how she phrased it.

We, and the crowd of black robes, metal skirts, shiny turbans, and dull-brown sheets, were glued to the duet that stood in the river.

John, in his hairy shirt, and Jesus, in a white robe, stared at each other as mud-clouded water meandered past.

You won't believe what happened next. A blast of thunder rumbled across the clear, blue sky. And while we could still hear it echoing down the river, a beam of light shown down from above, like a spotlight. It bounced off Jesus' shoulders in a thousand directions, causing everyone within eyeshot to squint.

When we could see clearly again, a pure white dove was perched on Jesus' right shoulder—where the light had first hit him.

Then the sky spoke. It spoke with a deep, resonant voice. This is what it said:

"This is my Son, chosen and marked by my love, delight of my life."[29]

FAMILY DISCUSSION

1. Has anyone ever called you the "delight of my life"?

2. How do you think Jesus felt when he heard his "real" Dad say that to him?

3. How would you want to act toward God if he called you the "delight of his life?"

SCENE EIGHTEEN
THE IMPRISONMENT OF JOHN[30]

The sky stopped talking; and the dove vanished from sight. Jesus was the only one present who didn't look like a frightened Chihuahua. He was as calm as a basset hound—it was as if he were used to having God proclaim his love, from high above. As if it were an everyday occurrence.

John slowly raised a hand and even more slowly reached over and touched Jesus on the cheek. He was looking at him like Mary had in the temple—eighteen human-years ago.

A smile stretched across the face of both Jesus and John, and then the smile turned into laughter and a bear hug. The crowd broke into applause.

Jesus and John let go of their grip and turned their beaming faces toward the multitude. Then Jesus patted John on his shoulders, twice, and spoke to him.

I'm not sure what he said, but it caused John to shake his head vigorously, from side to side, as if his neck were shouting, "No!" Jesus spoke to John again. John stared down at the water.

"Let's get a little closer," Pete said. "I can't hear them."

Jesna nodded, touched a button on the dash of the car, and we moved forward to the edge of the river.

"I'm not worthy to reach down and tie your shoe" was the first thing we heard John say. He continued. "I'm the one that needs to be baptized, not you!"

But Jesus insisted.

"Do it. God's work, putting things right all these centuries, is coming together right now in this baptism."[31]

John's head, this time slowly nodding, indicated his reluctant agreement. Then, he did it. He stepped around to the side of Jesus and laid God's Son back in the muddy water.

After the baptism, Jesus gave John a wet hug and made his way up from the river and back through the crowd, as water dripped from him to the dry ground. I halfway expected flowers to start springing up behind as he walked. But that didn't happen. This wasn't Disney. It was real.

Just before Jesus disappeared from view, John found his lost voice (I remembered that his father used to lose his voice). "That's the One!" John shouted. "He is the One I've been telling you about! That's the Messiah!"

"That may be, Baptist. But you're the one Herod sent us for." Those words came from the mouth of the leader of a group of metal-skirted soldiers. They were carrying swords and spears. The crowd parted in fear before their march. They stormed into the water, and it was clear that they were not looking for a baptism.

"Grab him," the lead marcher said. Two of them seized John by his arms and pushed them behind his back. "Herod wants a word with you," was all the leader said before leaving with John in tow.

Except for a couple of muffled "No's" the crowd was silent.

"Can't you help him, Jesna?" Priscilla asked.

"Yeah, can't we run over them with this car? I'll drive!" Pete added.

"What will they do to him?" asked Mrs. Pilgrim.

"There's nothing we can do to change history—especially Bible history. Preaching repentance is almost never the popular thing to do, particularly when you've been telling everyone about the sins of the king. Herod has sent for John. To shut him up."

FAMILY DISCUSSION

1. Why do you think Jesus wanted to be baptized by John?

2. How do you think it felt for John to dip God under the water he had created?

3. Have you ever, like John, been in trouble for doing the *right* thing?

SCENE NINETEEN
THE GENEALOGY OF JESUS[32]

We sat for a long time. The crowd began to thin. Then, Jesna started pushing buttons and, before you could say "Fetch!" we were moving at a rapid speed—through rocks, trees, the remains of the crowd, and the side of a camel. We even ran right through the pack of soldiers who had arrested John. They couldn't feel us, of course, not even a tickle. It did make Jesna smile a little, though.

We crested the rocky hill (big enough to keep the Jordan River confined, even during a monsoon). "Ouch!" said Priscilla as we bounced over a rock formation that looked like a giant hand lying across our path. "Why do we feel what we are riding over, but not what, ("or whom" Pete inserted) we are riding through?"

"I don't really know," Jesna said.

"Huh?" said Pete, "there is *something* you don't know?"

"I suppose," Jesna continued, "the ride was designed to be *realistic*, without, uh, being *fatalistic*."

"Huh?" Pete said again, scratching his head.

"It's supposed to be fun, Pete," Priscilla said, "but without killing anybody."

"Oh, I get it, it's like a cartoon... BUMP...Ouch! a cartoon that will bust your..."

"Pete." Mrs. Pilgrim said in a stern voice.

"...that will bust your backside."

Jesna giggled.

We descended into a green valley. "I think I smell olive oil," Mr. Pilgrim said.

"Popeye's wife?"

"No, Pete. Oil that comes from crushed olives," said Mr. Pilgrim.

I smelled it too, but it was nothing to bark about. In front of us was a town of stone and wood that had wrapped itself around the sides of a large hill. We raced toward it at the speed of a greyhound. In a matter of moments we had overtaken the town. The smooth surface of its streets were a welcome change from the bumping.

"This is the town of Nazareth," Jesna instructed. "This is where Jesus grew up."

"Look!" Pete hollered. "There he is now!"

Pete was right. Our car turned toward a small stone building.

We inched to a sand-grinding stop. In front of us Jesus, Mary, and Joseph sat facing each other in a triangle. They were sitting on small wooden stools just to the right of the doorway to the house. Brothers and sisters were standing around them. The smell of freshly cut wood was in the air for all to smell. I was probably the only one, however, who could smell the tears which were sliding down Mary's face, 'cause dogs can smell tears.

"We know you have to go now, Son," Joseph said, as he scratched at the ground with a stick. "Your mother and I have been preparing ourselves for this day since before you were even born."

"Since the angel told me about you," Mary added. "Since your father was told about you in a dream."

"So," Joseph continued, "we won't try to stop you—that would be as impossible as Noah stopping the flood. We just want you to know a few things before you go." Joseph caught himself looking at Jesus and quickly dropped his stare back down to the ground. In a moment he flung his head back up toward the sky. But it was too late to make his tears roll back upstream.

"Well, you know how your mother feels about you. And, uh, I want you to know that I couldn't love you any more if I had been your real father. So, leave here knowing that you are twice the son of God—by God, and through my lineage, as my adopted son. I am the son of Heli, son of Matthat, son of Levi, son of Melchi, son of Jannai, son of Joseph, son of Mattathias, son of Amos, son of Nathum, son of Esli, son of Naggai, son of Maath, son of Mattathias, son of Semein, son of Josech, son of Joda, son of Joanan, son of Rhesa, son of Zerubbabel, son of Shealtiel, son of Neri, son of Melchi, son of Addi, son of Cosam, son of Elmadam, son of Er, son of Joshua, son of Eliezer, son of Jorim, son of

Matthat, son of Levi, son of Simeon, son of Judah, son of Joseph, son of Jonam, son of Eliakim, son of Melea, son of Menna, son of Mattatha, son of Nathan, son of David, son of Jesse, son of Obed, son of Boaz, son of Sala, son of Nahshon, son of Amminadab, son of Admin, son of Arni, son of Hezron, son of Perez, son of Judah, son of Jacob, son of Isaac, son of Abraham, son of Terah, son of Nahor, son of Serug, son of Reu, son of Peleg, son of Eber, son of Shelah, son of Cainan, son of Arphaxed, son of Shem, son of Noah, son of Lamech, son of Methuselah, son of Enoch, son of Jared, son of Mahalaleel, son of Cainan, son of Enos, son of Seth, son of Adam, son of God."

Jesus had whispered each name as Joseph was saying them out loud. He had heard them before.

"So you, Jesus, are twice the son of God. And you will be the 'Father' to a whole new family."

FAMILY DISCUSSION

1. Have you ever had to say goodbye to someone you loved and would not see again for a long time?

2. What do you think Jesus was feeling when his parents were saying goodbye? What do you think his other Father was feeling?

SCENE TWENTY
THE TEMPTATION[33]

Jesus was the first to stand to his feet. Joseph followed and then Mary. There was a big, long-lasting, family hug. Then, Jesus backed slowly away from his earthly family, waved goodbye to his youth, turned, and followed the dusty path out of Nazareth.

"Where's he going?" Pete asked. Jesna was still studying Mary's face.

"He's going out into the desert, to prepare for a test."

"Jesus still has to take tests? He's still in school?"

"No, Pete. It's not a school test. He finished the last one of those before he got his first pimple. The devil is going to give him this test, and the whole universe is holding its breath, waiting for the results."

"If he passes it, do you think God will buy him a car? Dad said he would buy me a car if I ever make it out of high school."

"If Jesus passes this test," Jesna replied, "everybody in the universe wins a sixty-trillion dollar jackpot." That got Mr. Pilgrim's attention.

Jesna continued, as she was pushing buttons, "We'll catch up with him in about forty days."

Our Nazareth world of mostly brown colors began to spin around us like clothes in a washer on the spin cycle. When it stopped, I felt a little dizzy.

"I think I'm going to hurl," was Pete's response to all the motion.

"Don't talk about it!" said a pale Mr. Pilgrim.

"Look!" Mrs. Pilgrim gasped.

A few feet in front of us we saw Jesus, at least what was left of him. His dirty eyelids were tightly closed and his parched lips were moving with prayer. The desert had taken everything from him but skin-and-bone. His face was dark from the sun. His lips looked dry and painfully chapped. The bright clean robe he wore in Nazareth was now looking like the towel at the bottom of my dog-bed after a couple of months. His hair was dirty and matted.

He looked more like a slave's orphan than the
Universe-Creator's Son.

"Look over there," Priscilla said. "I
believe someone is coming to help him."

"Thank God!" said Mrs. Pilgrim. "He
looks pitiful."

A figure was approaching. As it drew near we could see that its
robe was so white it almost glowed, as did its face.

"Is that a man, a woman, or an angel?" asked Priscilla. "I can't
figure it out."

"Who cares if you can figure it out, Prissy," Pete jumped in,
"so long as it's... uh, he's going to help Jesus."

"That's not a man nor a woman," Jesna said. "But, 'he' was an
angel at one time. And, I assure you, he hasn't come to help.
That's the 'Prince of this World', the Devil, and he's come to give
Jesus the test he's been preparing for."

Just then the Devil, knowing Jesus must be starving, adminis-
tered the first test question, in a booming voice:

"Since you are God's Son, speak the word that will turn these
stones into loaves of bread."

Jesus looked up from where he sat praying. (He looked so
hungry the rock itself was enough to make him salivate.) He
squinted as he looked at the Devil's glowing face, and said in a
weak whisper:

"It takes more than bread to stay alive. It takes a steady stream
of words from God's mouth."

The Devil scowled and let out a tree-bending groan. But then a smile returned to his face, and he said, "Come with me."

"Let's go," Jesna said. In an instant we were, all eight of us, on the roof of a huge building. "We're on top of the Temple, in Jerusalem," Jesna whispered. The Holy City spread out around us about as far as you could see. Here came test question number two.

"Since you are God's Son, jump. He has placed you in the care of angels. They will catch you so that you won't so much as stub your toe on a stone."

"A stubbed toe can be pretty bad," Pete moaned a little at the thought.

"Shhhhh!" Priscilla looked annoyed.

Jesus responded, his voice weak and soft, but sure.

"Don't you dare test the Lord your God."

The Devil roared like a lion with a spear in its side. He began to wave his hands wildly, and then he and Jesus vanished. We followed them, after a few clicks of the buttons, to the peak of what must be the tallest mountain on the planet. The Devil's arms were still in motion. He was gesturing and pointing like an energetic tour guide. He spoke the third question, as he pointed out all the kingdoms of earth, and how glorious they were:

"They're yours lock, stock, and barrel. Just go down on your knees and worship me, and they're yours."

Jesus didn't even look up. He said, apparently in the strongest voice he could find in his dry throat:

"Beat it, Satan! [God's word says:] 'Worship the Lord your God, and only him. Serve him with absolute single-heartedness."[34]

With that the Devil was gone, in less than a New York second. In his place were more angels than you could fit in a hospital emergency room, all attending to the needs of Jesus.

"He passed!" Jesna shouted with glee.

"But what was the test, Jesna? And how do you pass it?" Priscilla asked sincerely.

The answer didn't come from Jesna. Gabriel looked up from the work he was doing and smiled at Priscilla. Then he spoke to her—to all of us.

"The test is the same one that humans have been flunking for 4,000 years, to resist the sugar-cookie crumbs of temptations that the Devil offers to your body, your mind, and your spirit. Your brother here," and he gave Jesus a tender look, "just passed with flying colors."

FAMILY DISCUSSION

1. What do you think it feels like to have gone for over a month without eating?

2. Why do you think it was important for Jesus to go out into the wilderness to fast and pray before he began his earthly ministry?

3. If you could have been with the angels, taking care of Jesus, what would you have said to him?

SCENE TWENTY-ONE
THE CALL OF THE FIRST DISCIPLES[35]

We left Jesus in the care of Gabriel and his emergency room staff of angels, and drove over, around, and through the barren wilderness that insulates the Holy Land of Israel like a Thermos bottle. Our many-miled trip came to an end at the northwest shore of the Sea of Galilee.

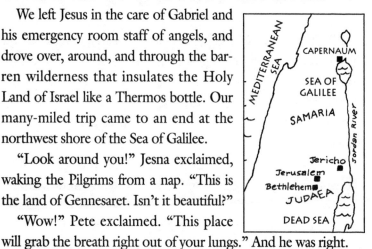

"Look around you!" Jesna exclaimed, waking the Pilgrims from a nap. "This is the land of Gennesaret. Isn't it beautiful?"

"Wow!" Pete exclaimed. "This place will grab the breath right out of your lungs." And he was right.

We were parked on the tip of a fertile green plain that had pushed its way out into the sparkling blue water of the Sea of Galilee. A range of rocky hills were in the distance, holding the water in place.

"Look how loamy this soil is," Jesna said.

"Look how what it is?" Pete asked, and turned toward his dad. "What's loamy, Dad?"

"The earth is very dark and rich and crumbly here," Dad answered.

"That's right," Jesna said and went on, "it's so fertile that there are fig trees, olive trees, palm trees, and walnut trees all growing here. This is probably the only place on the planet that all four of those trees grow together."

"I bet the garden of Sweden looked just like this place."

"That's Eden, Garden of Eden, Pete. Goodnight! What do you do during Sunday school, anyway, peel glue off your hands and daydream?" Priscilla was really disgusted with him.

"I don't put glue on my hands, Prissy, although it *is* fun to pull off."

Jesna pushed a giggle back and tickled me behind the ear. Then she pushed a few buttons which started time swirling again.

When it stopped, Jesus was standing in front of us with his sandled feet pressing into the sandy shore of the Sea of Galilee. A small crowd had circled around him. Now they listened to him talk.

"Wow, he sure looks better now," Pete said for all of us. "Them angels are real miracle workers."

"*Those* angels are real miracle workers, Pete," Mrs. Pilgrim said.

"Yeah, Mom, that's what I said."

Behind Jesus, two boats made from planks were tied to the shore with thick, hairy ropes. Four fishermen were standing knee-deep in water and scrubbing their nets. They seemed to be listening to Jesus as they worked. Then Jesus turned from the crowd and looked in their direction.

"Hey, you there. Do you mind if I stand in one of your boats so these people can hear me better?"

The four fishermen shrugged their shoulders. Then one of them, the one with the thickest hair and beard, invited Jesus into his boat by pointing with his head. Jesus walked through the water and climbed onto the head-pointing-fisherman's boat. The fisherman offered his shoulder for Jesus to use to steady himself as he climbed aboard.

"That's Simon Peter," Jesna whispered.

Jesus continued his talk as if there was nothing unusual about preaching from a floating pulpit or using water as a microphone. The crowd, including all four fishermen, became transfixed.

"Hey, he doesn't have an English accent like those, what do you call them, 'Shakespeare-Jesuses' in the movies."

Priscilla looked at her brother as if his head had suddenly turned purple.

"No, Pete," Jesna said, "he's got a Nazareth accent, and he's speaking Aramaic. The only reason you can understand him at all is because I set the special translation feature of the ride. That's his real voice you are hearing, but you hear it in English."

"I hear it in American."

Then, without even telling a funny story or taking up an offering, Jesus turned to the thick-haired fisherman and said:

"Push out into deep water and let your nets out for a catch."

Simon Peter spoke back:

"Master, we've been fishing hard all night and haven't caught even a minnow. But if you say so, I'll let out the nets."

As soon as the boat had traveled back out into deeper water, the two fishermen in the boat slung their black fishing nets out across the fluorescent-blue water. And, before you could say "Chihuahua," the nets sank and captured a huge haul of slimy, flapping, splashing fish that caused the nets to be strained to capacity.

"Get out here! Now!" the lead fisherman screamed to the two who had stayed by the shore. Within minutes both boats were surrounded by the green, wiggling catch. Jesus threw his head back and laughed in delight at the sight of the four frantic fishermen. The crowd cheered as if they were at a football game. It took all the experience the fishermen had to bring their two boats back to shore without having them swamped. When the boats were secured, Jesus climbed down.

But Simon Peter left the fish to his friends and raced after Jesus. He fell to his knees in front of him and, as water dripped from his nose and ears, said:

"Master, leave. I'm a sinner and can't handle this holiness. Leave me to myself."

Then Jesus spoke to him as he gently touched Simon Peter's sun-baked hair:

"There is nothing to fear. From now on you'll be fishing for men and women."[36]

Jesus turned and walked away. Simon Peter ran back to his four friends. They all spoke excitedly, all at the same time. The only thing I could make out was when Simon Peter shouted, "Yes, let's do it!"

Then he turned to the open-mouthed crowd and shouted. "Enjoy the fish, they're all yours."

With that, the four began sprinting up the beach, following the footsteps Jesus had left in the sand. They were off to become disciples of the Master Fisherman. They were his first catch.

FAMILY DISCUSSION

1. What do you think Jesus meant when he told Peter that he would be fishing for men and women?

2. What do you think Peter and the other three fishermen were feeling when they left their careers lying on the lake shore and ran off to follow a man they had only known for a few minutes?

3 .What would you say if Jesus came to your front door and said, "Follow me"?

SCENE TWENTY-TWO
THE MARRIAGE AT CANA[37]

For the next three Bible-days we drove around through countryside. At first we circled the huge lake, called Lake Gennesaret or Galilee, where Jesus had spoken. We watched the sun set and rise again on its face, making more colors than an artist's palette could possibly hold. Then we drove west, up into the highlands of Galilee, to the small village of Cana. Along the way Jesna began to tell us about the next time we would see Jesus—at a wedding.

"Is Jesus getting married?" Pete asked.

"No," Jesna replied. "He and his mother will be guests at a wedding."

"Will he be wearing a tux?"

"No. Probably the same dusty robe you saw him wearing at the lake."

"How much older will he be? Will he have grey hair?"

"He'll be three days older and he won't have grey hair."

"Does he use Grecian Formula, like Dad?"

"That'll be enough questions, Pete," said Dad as he laid his hand on his son's shoulder.

Priscilla must have thought that meant it was her turn to start. "How long will the wedding last? I know in our church they last about forty-seven minutes, not counting the part where you eat cake and try to catch the bouquet. That's another fifty-two minutes."

"Well, Priscilla, weddings are very different here in first-century Israel. They're a whole lot more spectacular. Unlike the weddings you've seen, there is no religious ceremony. That happens earlier, with the betrothal. That's when they become engaged. On the day of the wedding the bride gets all dressed up. She wears a white robe with all kinds of jewels and embroidery on it. She also wears a veil over her face and a garland in her hair. She looks as much like an angel as a human can. And she waits for the groom at her house. The bridegroom, along with his friends, musicians, and singers, goes to her house."

"And I bet she doesn't come out the first time he honks the horn."

"Donkeys don't have horns, *l-i-t-t-le* brother."

"Yeah, well cows do."

"As I was saying," Jesna giggled, "the groom arrives and receives the bride from her parents. Then, the whole party goes back to the groom's house for a celebration, where there is a whole lot of music, dancing, joking, and laughter. The wedding party can last from one to two weeks. There's really nothing in your world to compare it to. It is a BIG deal. A BIG celebration."

"Sounds bigger than the Superbowl!" Pete added.

As Jesna was putting a period on her last sentence, we came to a stop. We parked in an enormous, open courtyard. Sandstone slabs, as far as the eye could see (at least in the lantern-lit night) were beneath us. There were small trees, clay pots of flowers, wooden tables, and hundreds of swirling, twirling people all around. Music filled the warm night air. Then we heard someone talking in low tones. The person was standing right beside us.

"This is terrible. I can't believe it. I'll never be able to look my friends in the face again. I'm host- ing the wedding party of the decade, and we have just run out of wine. The groom will kill me. He really will kill me." He was talking to a man who was also wearing panic for makeup.

"Excuse me, sir." It was Mary, Jesus' mother.

 "Look!" cried Pete.

"We know. We know."

"My name is Mary."

"I knew it!" shouted Pete.

"And I wasn't trying to overhear your conversation, but I think I... I mean... my Son might be able to help you. He's very special."

"Not unless he owns a wine cellar," said the oversized man, with sparkly, ring-covered fingers. "Or, unless he can turn water into wine."

"Well, sir, that's exactly what he *can* do."

"Yeah," said the man, in a sarcastic voice. "Why don't you run along and tell him to do that. And tell him to turn some stones into cheese while he's at it."

Mary smiled kindly and walked away.

Within moments, some men were lining up six stone pots in the center of the courtyard. Jesus was there, telling the men what to do.

"Look," Jesna said. "Those are large pots are used in the Jewish purification ceremony."

"They're huge," Priscilla said. "By my calculations," and she paused to make a few last punches on her wrist computer, "each will hold twenty to thirty gallons."

"Fill them to the brim with water," Jesus said, in a sure voice.

The helpers did as he asked. "Now," Jesus said, "dip the pitchers in and serve the wine."

The men gave each other puzzled looks, but did as they were told. Jesus whispered to one of the men and pointed in the direction of the host. The man took his overflowing pitcher to the big man with the sparkling fingers. He looked a little angry and even more puzzled. But he poured from the pitcher into his metal cup and tipped the cup to his bejowled mouth. When he brought the cup away from his mouth, he let out a loud "Ahhhh!" and then smiled a broad smile that turned into a belly laugh.

Then, he exclaimed in a loud voice, "Everybody I know begins with their finest wines and after the guests have had their fill brings in the cheap stuff. But you," he said, looking at the bridegroom, "have saved the best till now!"

The crowd erupted in applause and laughter. I'm not sure what the host would have thought if he had heard Pete say, "Care for some cheese?"

FAMILY DISCUSSION

1. Why do you think that Jesus performed his first miracle at a wedding?

2. When you hear this story, what do you think of Jesus' miracle working power?

TWENTY-THREE
THE SOJOURN AT CAPERNAUM[38]

After the wedding, Jesus went down from Cana to Capernaum, with his mother and his disciples.

We followed closely behind. Something about being with Jesus, in between the lines of the Bible as he made dust clouds in the sand with his sandled feet, laughed with his friends, and stopped the caravan to smell a flower, made the words of the Bible come alive. I think Pete had the same thought.

"You know," he said, "I think this movie is a whole lot better than the book."

"How would you know? You've never read it," Priscilla taunted.

"Well, I've heard the preacher read from it. And this is a whole lot less boring. It's even fun."

"Jesna," Mr. Pilgrim said in a thoughtful voice, "Wasn't that Jesus' first miracle? The wedding in Cana?"

"That's right. Turning water into wine at a wedding feast was the first miracle of Jesus.... Uh... well... at least the first one the Bible tells us about."

"Oh!" said Pete. "You mean Jesus might have decided to hit a baseball for a thousand-foot home run in one of his Little League games in Nazareth."

"No, that's not what I meant."

"Well," Mr. Pilgrim continued, "it didn't seem to be that spectacular, given that it was his first one, and all. I don't mean to be disrespectful but..."

"Yeah," Pete interrupted. "Why didn't he make one of those mean ole Roman soldiers drop dead and then come back to life again, or make a donkey fly or talk, or something? That would have gotten a lot more attention."

Jesna's eyes began to twinkle as if she had been waiting for this question.

"It's important to remember a couple of things about Jesus. First, he came to this world from a place that no human has ever been—the kingdom of heaven. He wants to get people excited about that place. But, since people have never been there, they don't have words to use about it. So Jesus has to use stories and pictures and miracles as ways to teach them about a place they have never seen and to encourage them to live a way that they have never tried. Secondly, Jesus is a master teacher. He never wastes an opportunity to help people learn."

"Priscilla, how many gallons of water did you say those earthen pots held?"

"About twenty to thirty. Why?"

"Well, can you think of any other earthen pots that hold about that much water?"

"Any pot could be made that size," Priscilla said, a little impatiently, as she punched the buttons on her wrist computer. Then, suddenly, she stopped. "Hey, I just thought of something!" People are like earthen containers filled with gallons of water."

"I think I get it," said Mr. Pilgrim. "Jesus has come to..."

"Turn our water off, Dad?"

"No! To change the contents of our earthen containers, our lives, into something new."

"That's right, Mr. Pilgrim," said Jesna. "To put new life in these old earthen pots. To change us from the inside out. And that should be the most joyous occasion you can imagine."

"Like a wedding?" Priscilla asked.

"Yes. Like a first-century Jewish wedding. His church is the bride. And he is the groom who has thrown the party."

"And he's the one who turns our water into wine," Pete added.

"Wow!" said Priscilla, still staring at her wrist. "How did I miss that?"

FAMILY DISCUSSION

1. What does it mean to be an "earthen pot"?

2. What do you think it means to have yourself changed into something new?

3. How would a person filled with Jesus' "new wine" act differently from someone who is just a plain-old water pot?

SCENE TWENTY-FOUR
THE FIRST JOURNEY TO JERUSALEM[39]

Capernaum was in sight. It was a beautiful town of stone buildings, laughing children, and barking dogs, nestled on the northwest shore of the Sea of Galilee.

"This is the town that will serve as Jesus' headquarters for the next three years during his ministry."

"Three years!" Pete groaned. "I'll never make it."

"That's three Bible-years," Jesna said, with a reassuring tone. "That's only a few stomach-seconds for you."

"That's just what I mean," said Pete.

"It's easy to see why he would pick this place," Mrs. Pilgrim interrupted. "It looks as if it belongs on a picture postcard."

And she was right. The sparkling blue of the sea, which lay in front of the town like a giant welcome mat, the sandy brown earth tones of the village, the splashes of April green of the surrounding countryside, and all the vibrant reds, yellows, and purples of the street vendors were breathtaking.

"This is a pretty good sized town," Pete said. "Do you think we'll be able to go to the Capernaum Mall while we're here?"

"Sure we will, Pete," Jesna said. "Almost every downtown street is a shopping mall. I just hope you like fish, though, because that's the main thing to buy here."

Jesna continued, "Capernaum is big enough to have its own synagogue, ah… ah, church, and its own tax-collecting station for the Roman Empire."

"Yeah," Pete said, "it would make a couple of Nazareths with a Cana left over."

We spent the next few days hanging close to Jesus and his small band of disciples. I think that if I weren't allowed to live with the Pilgrims, I would most like to live in Capernaum. With all the fish in the marketplaces, there were more cats around than a thousand dogs could ever chase.

Our few days in Capernaum quickly came to an end—too quickly for me. Then Jesna announced it was time to follow Jesus and his friends down south to Jerusalem. She said we would be there in time for the celebration of the Feast of the Passover.

"I know what a feast is, Jesna," Pete said. "But what's a Passover feast? It sounds like you might not get to eat anything, if you're passing it over."

"The Passover, or the Feast of Unleavened Bread, as it is sometimes called, is the first of seven annual feasts the Jewish people celebrate each year. It's the most important one, because it is when the Jews stop and remember how God delivered them from Egypt and established them as the nation of Israel."

"But why is the bread unlevitated?" Pete asked. "That doesn't sound very tasty."

"The bread is 'unleavened,' which means it doesn't have yeast in it to make it rise. The Jewish people had to leave Egypt in such a hurry that there wasn't time to wait for the yeast to do its work," Jesna answered.

"How far did you say it was to Jerusalem? Why is Jesus going to walk all that way to eat flat bread?"

"Jerusalem is a little over a hundred miles south of Capernaum, Pete [see map on page 76]. And Jesus is going there because he is a male Jew. It's part of his religious beliefs."

"But," Mr. Pilgrim said, "do all the men have to go to Jerusalem to celebrate it?"

"No, Mr. Pilgrim. He wouldn't have to go all the way to Jerusalem, but I guess he wanted to officially start his earthly ministry in the Holy City by celebrating the deliverance of his people. After all, deliverance of people in bondage is what his whole ministry is about. And he is the 'Bread of Life' that they will need to eat to be free."

"And the new wine he already made, back in Cana. Right, Jesna?"

A wide, radiant smile spread across Jesna's face. "That's exactly right, Pete. You're a quick student of living parables."

FAMILY DISCUSSION

1. How do you think Jesus felt as he made his way to Jerusalem, to officially start his ministry on earth?

2. If you could have been walking with him, what would you have said to encourage him?

3. What do you think Jesna meant by saying Jesus is the "Bread of Life" that people need to eat to be free?

SCENE TWENTY-FIVE
THE CLEANSING OF THE TEMPLE[40]

It took ten days to do it, but we completed the trip from Capernaum to Jerusalem. We followed closely behind Jesus and his band of friends every step of the way, as they walked, talked, and laughed around crackling campfires, ate oversized biscuits of bread, and slept under a canopy of stars.

Once Pete said, "Life's just one big camping trip for Jesus, isn't it?" His dad didn't say anything in response, but judging by the relaxed smile on his face, it sure appeared that he'd like to try it for a while.

In the early afternoon of the tenth day of our journey, we could see we were approaching a huge city. It was spread out over a hillside like a sandy brown quilt with a few patches of dark green dots. Jesus and his disciples seemed to become more serious as they came closer to the city.

"Isn't it beautiful?" Jesna whispered. "That's the Holy City—Jerusalem."

Soon we could see that the city was surrounded by a high stone wall. Pete was the first to comment on it.

"That's a pretty serious fence they have around that place. There must be some important stuff in there."

After a couple of hours had passed from our first spotting of Jerusalem, we found ourselves following Jesus and his disciples right through a large gateway in the huge rock wall that kept the city from spilling out into the countryside.

"If somebody fell off that wall they'd be dead, wouldn't they, Dad?"

"Probably so, son."

"Yeah, I bet a cat would use up one of its lives if it fell off that wall."

I liked the sound of that.

Inside the walls, the city was a beehive of activity. Mr. Pilgrim said there were more people in the streets than there were in the streets of New York City, five minutes after quitting time. Fortunately, we were able to drive right through them, or we would never have been able to keep up with Jesus.

When he finally stopped, we were standing at the entrance to an enormous courtyard. The courtyard was paved with sandstone blocks and mortar. It spread out before us like a patio at a giant's house. It was bordered by a procession of stone archways, each supported by columns, carved from stone. Mrs. Pilgrim called them a "colonnade."

"Hey look!" Pete shouted, "Isn't that the building we crashed through when we saw Jesus dedicated? I didn't know this big ole patio went with it."

The patio did go with it. And it was filled with people, cattle, sheep, and cages and cages of birds. The noise they all made was a loud roar. It looked like everybody there was trying to sell something to everybody else. The place was an outdoor mall, cattle auction, and Wall Street, all tossed together in a giant salad of noise, smell, and jangling coins.

I followed Jesna's eyes to Jesus. For the first time since we had first seen him in Bethlehem, he looked angry. He was wrapping long strips of leather together while his disciples stood around with "don't-do-it" looks on their faces.

"Look," Pete said, "He's making a craft to sell, like everybody else is doing."

"Nope," was all Jesna said back.

Within moments the strips had been fashioned into a long whip. And no sooner was it fashioned than it was put to work. Jesus became a one-man wrecking crew. He began to crack the whip and chase the merchants out of the courtyard. He stampeded the sheep and cattle, upended tables, caused a thousand birds to break out of their cages and fly in ten thousand different directions. He sent coins flying like hail, and he was the wind in the hailstorm. He only paused once, to shout for all to hear:

"Get your things out of here! Stop turning my Father's house into a shopping mall!"

After a few cracks of his whip, Jesus began to calm his own storm. He let the whip rest behind his neck and turned in a slow circle to inspect his handiwork. He seemed neither pleased nor displeased, just lost in thought. Except for a few confused sheep, a handful of bewildered disciples, and several huddles of men, the courtyard was quiet and empty.

The quiet was short-lived. A group of men with black robes and tall black hats marched out of the shadows of the colonnade and came to where Jesus stood. Behind them was another group, a small band of red-faced merchants. The lead black robe asked:

"What credentials can you present to justify this?"

Jesus answered, "Tear down this Temple and in three days I'll put it back together."

They were indignant: "It took forty-six years to build this Temple, and you're going to rebuild it in three days?"[41]

Jesus said nothing more. His stare melted into a look of sadness and compassion. Then he turned to his disciples, and nodded that it was time to leave. He let the leather whip slide from his shoulders to the stone floor as he turned and walked from the temple. The courtyard had become so quiet that the sound of a coin dropping would've seemed like an explosion. His Father's house was stone silent, as it should be.

FAMILY DISCUSSION

1. Did you know that in Scripture your body is referred to as the temple of the Holy Spirit?

2. How do you feel inside when you are quiet like a "house of prayer"? How do you feel when everything inside seems filled with noise and activity like Jesus found in the Temple?

3. What can you do to help Jesus turn your own temple (body) into *his* house?

SCENE TWENTY-SIX
JESUS' MINISTRY IN JERUSALEM[42]

"Will we be going to jail now?" Pete asked Jesna.

"To jail, Pete? No. Why do you ask?"

"Well, we've been with Jesus where ever he goes, and, I'm sure they'll be putting him in jail for disturbing the peace, or assault with a deadly whip, or something."

"I see your point, Pete," Jesna said as she surveyed the topsy-turvy temple courtyard. "And, I'm sure that a lot of those" (she motioned with her head to a small group of black-robed, angry-faced men huddled together by the entrance to the Temple) "Pharisees would love to do just that."

"Then why don't they?" Pete asked.

"Well, for one thing, they don't run the jails. The Romans do. You see, Pete, Jerusalem, and all of Israel, is under the control of the Roman Empire. It's the Romans who make the rules, and the Romans who decide on punishment when the laws are broken. They would probably consider what Jesus did today to be a religious matter and of little consequence to the Empire."

"So, the Empire won't be striking back."

"No, Pete. We'll be with Jesus when he celebrates the Passover, or the Feast of Unleavened Bread. The celebration will be going on for seven more days."

"Where can I buy a calendar, Jesna?" Pete asked.

Priscilla perked up at that. "You want to keep up with time, little brother!?"

"I sure do. If we're supposed to be feasting for seven whole days I want to make sure the people throwing the party don't try to cheat us out of one of the days. Ya'know, we've already seen them run out of supplies at one party."

"Oh, Pete!" Jesna said smiling. "You surely remind me of a one-stringed guitar."

"Huh?"

"There are no calendars here. At least nothing like what you are used to. On the old Jewish calendar, though, it's the 14th of Nisan."

"The Jewish people name their months after Japanese cars?"

"No, Pete, we're still two millennia away from there being any cars."

"Two millennia? Are you talking about a car again? Ouch!" Priscilla was slowly dislodging her elbow from Pete's ribs.

"Nisan, which is the same as April, is the first month of the religious year. On the 14th day of that month—that's today—the Jews celebrate Passover. That is, they commemorate the deliverance of their ancestors from Egypt and the establishment of Israel as a nation. They're celebrating God's love for them.

"Tomorrow," Jesna continued, "well, actually, at sundown tonight, they will begin a seven-day celebration of 'The Feast of Unleavened Bread.'"

"Yeah, you've already told us about that unlevitated bread," Pete interrupted.

"We'll be with Jesus as he celebrates with his disciples, and the Jews in Jerusalem. It's an exciting time. He'll begin to do even more signs and miracles, to prove to the people that he has a right to speak as God's Son. But…" Jesna continued in a softer voice, "he'll be cautious of their praise. He knows very well what is in the hearts of men."

As she said this, her eyes swept around the colonnade, which was still littered with coins, broken cages, and the overturned wares of a legion of merchants.

FAMILY DISCUSSION

1. What do you think was going through the minds of the disciples as they were watching Jesus clear the temple?

2. How do you think Pete and Priscilla felt as they watched?

3. How would you explain Jesus' behavior in clearing the temple to someone who had never read the story before?

SCENE TWENTY-SEVEN
THE DISCOURSE WITH NICODEMUS[43]

After seven days of feasting and miracles, we
found ourselves sitting
with Jesus and his dis-
ciples at their base camp—a

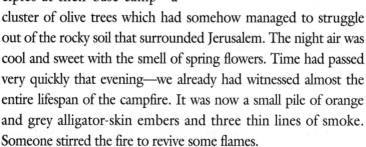

cluster of olive trees which had somehow managed to struggle
out of the rocky soil that surrounded Jerusalem. The night air was
cool and sweet with the smell of spring flowers. Time had passed
very quickly that evening—we already had witnessed almost the
entire lifespan of the campfire. It was now a small pile of orange
and grey alligator-skin embers and three thin lines of smoke.
Someone stirred the fire to revive some flames.

As the latest round of laughter was beginning to fade, the
sound of approaching footsteps was heard—first by me (because
dogs hear better than people), then by those with the best human
ears, then by all. We looked and saw a very strange sight.

One of the black-robed men stood within the glow of firelight.
His fine clothes, carefully curled hair, and smell (there was none)
seemed as out of place as would be a closely cropped poodle running with a pack of junkyard dogs.

The man broke the silence:

"Rabbi, we all know you are a teacher straight from God. No
one could do all the God-pointing, God-revealing acts you do
if God weren't in on it."

I heard one of the disciples whisper while he was talking, "Did
you hear that? Nicodemus, a member of the ruling elders, called

Jesus 'Rabbi'?" He seemed very impressed by that, but Jesus didn't. When the man finished, Jesus said:

"You're absolutely right. Take it from me: unless a person is born from above, it's not possible to see what I'm pointing to—to God's kingdom."

Nicodemus look puzzled, as if he had been right about something and he hadn't known what he had said. He replied:

"How can anyone be born who has already been born and grown up?"

"Good question!" Pete said, a little too loudly.

"You can't re-enter your mother's womb and be born again. What are you saying with this 'born-from-above' talk?"

Jesus said, "You're not listening."

Several of the disciples gasped and looked like frightened gerbils when he said that to Nicodemus.

"Let me say it again. Unless a person submits to this original creation—the 'wind hovering over the water' creation, the invisible moving the visible, a baptism into a new life—it's not possible to enter God's kingdom. When you look at a baby, it's just that: a body you can look at and touch. But the person who takes shape within is formed by something you can't see and touch—the Spirit—and becomes a living spirit.

"So don't be surprised when I tell you that you have to be 'born from above'—out of this world, so to speak."[44]

Jesus and Nicodemus continued to talk. After a while, Jesna whispered an explanation. "You see, even though Nicodemus is a great teacher and a leader among the Pharisees, he doesn't grasp the first-grade-level basics about spiritual life or about God's love."

"But I don't get it," Pete said. "Why did God make it so hard that wise, old teachers can't even figure it out?"

"Pete," Jesna said in the kindest voice, "it's not that it's so hard. It's that it's *so easy*. Have you ever read *Cinderella*?"

"Yep," said Pete. "But it would have been a whole lot more better if some superheroes—with all kinds of special powers—had been in it, instead of that 'fairy godmother.'"

"Well, Pete," Jesna said, "imagine that *Cinderella*, a story only a few pages long, was written with a thousand footnotes. Do you know what a footnote is?"

"Yea. It's the BSBB."

"What?"

"The Boring-Stuff-at-the-Bottom-of-the-Book."

"Oh! Now, imagine that the Cinderella story had about four hundred pages of 'BSBB', and that Nicodemus had become an expert in all the footnotes. Imagine he could tell you how much the pumpkin weighed to the nearest centigram."

"And the oldest step-sister's middle name," Pete interrupted.

"Yes, that too. But, suppose he had been studying the footnotes so long that he had forgotten the story. Forgotten that the story is about a prince searching his kingdom for a bride—unable to conceive the notion that there might be a prince right there who is searching his kingdom for people to live with him in his palace. That's what Jesus is trying to tell him, that the real story is very simple and has him, Nicodemus, as one of the main characters.

Listen to what he is saying," and she pointed toward Jesus.

"This is how much God loved the world: He gave his Son, his one and only Son. And this is why: so that no one need be destroyed; by believing in him, anyone can have a whole and lasting life."[45]

After they had finished speaking, Nicodemus reached out and gave Jesus' hand a squeeze. But then he quickly spun around and walked away from the light of the fire and away from God's Son back into the dark of night. Jesus held back a tear as he turned and took his seat by the smoldering fire.

"Do you know what the name Nicodemus means?" Jesna asked. All four pilgrims and I shook our heads.

"It means 'victor over the people.' Tonight he almost found victory over himself. But that will have to wait for a while."

Pete shot Jesna a curious look and then peered up the trail. "I bet he is looking for a glass sandal."

FAMILY DISCUSSION

1. How could Jesus expect a grown man like Nicodemus to be born again?

2. Do you understand what it means to be born again—to be able to see and live in God's kingdom?

3. What do you suppose kept Nicodemus from being willing to be a part of God's kingdom?

SCENE TWENTY-EIGHT
JESUS' MINISTRY IN JUDEA[46]

The next morning, after Jesus' conversation with Nicodemus, he and the disciples broke camp and went into the Judean countryside. Jesna told us that "Judea" was a block of land that formed an almost perfect sixty-mile by sixty-mile square. (Actually, she said one hundred kilometers by one hundred kilometers, but Priscilla did the conversions for the rest of us.) She explained that the thick, salty water of the Dead Sea forms most of Judea's eastern boundary and that the teeming-with-life Mediterranean Sea confines it on the west. In the middle of the square is a backbone of "Judean Hills."

It was in these hills that we saw the most amazing sight—the Son of God playing with his friends.

On the second day of the vacation, Mr. Pilgrim spoke up. "You know, there is a lot I need to learn from Jesus."

Shock contorted the faces of the other three Pilgrims into fleshy question marks and I thought *Oh boy, maybe he'll find time to play fetch with me.* Jesna, however, looked at him as if he had said, "You know, I think humans should eat food to stay alive."

He went on, "Here is someone who's on loan from heaven, on a mission to save the world. Yet, he doesn't even start until he's thirty years old and now, he almost never seems to be in a hurry. He spends hours in prayer each day, and most of the rest of the time laughing and enjoying his friends."

"Yeah, Dad," Pete chimed in, "about the only time he hasn't been laughing or smiling is when he was kicking bullies out of the Temple."

"So, Mr. Pilgrim, what are you learning from Jesus?"

"I'm not sure yet, Jesna, but I sure would like to be more relaxed and happy and confident, like he is."

"He wasn't that relaxed in the Temple, Dad. I mean he was mad."

"We know, Pete, we know," Priscilla said. "We were there too, you might recall."

"Pete, do you remember what Mark Twain said?" Jesna asked.

"Mark who?"

"Mark *Twain,* dumbo!" Priscilla interrupted. "You know, the famous writer. He wrote *Tom Sawyer.*"

"Oh yeah," said Pete, "the white-haired guy with the cigar."

Jesna continued. "Mark Twain said, 'Show me someone who knows what's funny, and I'll show you someone who knows what isn't.'"

"So what do comedians have to do with Jesus?" Pete said.

"Everything, Pete. Jesus knows what is fun. Being in relationship with his friends and with his Father—that's fun. He also knows what isn't fun or funny: People being so preoccupied with money, power, and their own selfish interests, that they don't have time for relationships. The Temple in Jerusalem is where God's children go to express their loving relationship with their Father. They are to enjoy being with him, as the disciples are doing, right now, right over there. But the Temple was no longer a house of warmth and prayer. It had become a shopping mall. Jesus knew that wasn't funny. So, he brought his disciples out here to relax with him and to show them how things should be.

"He'll also do a little baptizing before he takes them back to work. He'll want to make sure they understood all that 'new birth' talk he'd had with Nicodemus. He'll want to lift them from the water, born again, and into a whole new way of living."

Mr. Pilgrim silently nodded his head.

FAMILY DISCUSSION

1. How much time does your family spend enjoying the two supreme commandments—loving God and loving neighbors (including each other)?

2. Try an experiment this week. Take a weekly calendar and block out at least five hours for practicing the two supreme commandments: loving God and loving others. Then, enjoy each of the 300 minutes you have set aside for fun.

SCENE TWENTY-NINE
JOHN'S TESTIMONY TO CHRIST[47]

It wasn't long until people began to trickle out from the cities, down through the valleys of the Judean hills, to be baptized by Jesus' disciples. And, in even less time, that trickle widened into a steady flow of dusty-footed humanity. It was enough to keep the disciples busy and Jesus smiling for the sunlit part of each day.

"Wow!" Pete announced, in the middle of what had been a long silence. "I believe Jesus' disciples are dunking more people than John the Baptist."

Jesna smiled, then said, "Let's take a drive." And that was all that was needed to send the four Pilgrims and me piling into the car.

"Where are we going?" Pete asked.

"We're going to see what John the Baptist is up to," Jesna responded.

"But, uh," Priscilla inserted, "I thought he was in prison."

"That's a little confusing, Priscilla. While John will very soon be in Herod's prison, he and his disciples are right now baptizing over at Aenon—it's a town near Salim that is known for its springs of water."

"Is he competing with Jesus? You know, like McDonald's and Wendy's? Are they having a baptism war?"

"No, Pete," Jesna laughed, "but it's funny you asked that. Hold on."

And hold on we did. I think we set a new record in the mile and five-mile, as Jesna turned the Judean countryside into a giant roller coaster track. Three of the Pilgrims held on with white knuckles and clenched eyes. Pete held his hands high over his head and squealed like a pig at a birthday party. Then in an instant our car stopped on a dime—while our bodies stopped on a ten-dollar bill. Standing inches in front of us was John the Baptist—I would recognize the scent of his camel skin shirt anywhere—and a semicircle of his disciples.

One of the disciples was speaking:

"Rabbi, you know the one who was with you on the other side of the Jordan? The one you authorized with your witness? Well, he's now competing with us." ["I told you." Pete whispered.] "He's baptizing, too, and everyone's going to him instead of us."

A quick 360-degree scanning of the countryside did reveal that the crowd around John was a fraction of the throng we had just left. We heard John answer his disciple:

"It's not possible for a person to succeed—I'm talking about *eternal* success—without heaven's help. You yourselves were there when I made it public that I was not the Messiah but simply the one sent ahead of him to get things ready. The one who gets the bride is, by definition, the bridegroom. And the bridegroom's friend, his 'best man'—that's me—in place at his side where he can hear every word, is genuinely happy. How could he be jealous when he knows that the wedding is finished and the marriage is off to a good start?

"That's why my cup is running over. This is the assigned moment for him to move into the center, while I slip off to the sidelines.

"...Whoever accepts and trusts the Son gets in on everything, life complete and forever! And that is also why the person who avoids and distrusts the Son is in the dark and doesn't see life. All he experiences of God is darkness, and an angry darkness at that."[48]

When John finished, the outspoken disciple quickly put away the anger that had been on his face, like a child hastily hiding a stolen cookie behind his back.

"Uh, Jesna," Pete said sheepishly, "so this isn't competition like McDonald's and Wendy's."

"No, Pete. It's more like the owner of a luxury cruise ship (which offers seven banquet feasts each day) and one of his travel agents."

"Oh."

FAMILY DISCUSSION

1. What do you think John the Baptist meant when he said that a person cannot truly succeed without "heaven's help"?

2. How do you suppose John can feel that his "cup is running over" (in other words, he is extremely happy) when he is going off to the sidelines, instead of being the first-string player?

3. Tomorrow, try to be genuinely happy when someone else is successful.

SCENE THIRTY
THE JOURNEY TO GALILEE[49]

"We're off!" Jesna said. And off we were. This time we rode the roller coaster backwards to where we had last seen Jesus and his disciples. But they, and most of the mass of people, were gone.

"Where is everybody?" Pete asked.

"He and the disciples are heading north, back to Galilee. We'll catch up with them before nightfall."

"But why did they leave?" Priscilla asked. "Things were going so well."

"Jesus just found out that John's disciples weren't the only ones keeping score on all the baptizing," Jesna answered. "The Pharisees have been keeping close tabs on both Jesus and John. And they don't know what John knows—that it's not a competition. They've been trying to turn Jesus and John into rivals in the eyes of the people. Jesus wants none of that. He has decided to get out of their territory for a while."

"Jesna," Mr. Pilgrim spoke up, "why do you think Jesus spends so much time in Galilee? I mean, I know its pretty there—it reminds me of Southern California, without the smog. But Judea is where Jerusalem and the Temple are located."

"You're very perceptive, Mr. Pilgrim." That put a glow on Mr. Pilgrim's face that could light an airport runway.

"Do you know the story of the divided kingdom?" Jesna asked.

All four Pilgrims shook their heads. I tried to shake my head too, but Mr. Pilgrim said, "Sit still, girl."

"Well, about 900 years ago, after Solomon's son, Rehoboam, became king in Jerusalem, Jeroboam led the northern tribes in rebellion. The kingdom divided into two parts—a southern part, Judah which contained Jerusalem, and a northern part, Israel."

"I'm sure I'll get that mixed up, Jesna," Pete chimed in. "Which one of the Boam boys was related to Solomon?"

Jesna giggled. "Rehoboam."

"And that's another reason I wonder why he spends so much time in the north," Mr. Pilgrim added. "If his bloodline, you know... his earthly family runs through the southern kingdom, why doesn't he stay there more?"

Jesna continued, "Two hundred years after Solomon died and after the kingdom was divided, the ten northern tribes were captured by the Assyrians. Those tribes became known as the 'ten lost tribes,' and disappeared completely from history. Judah, the southern kingdom, lasted for just under 140 years before it fell to Nebuchadnezzar. The walls of Jerusalem, the palaces, and the Temple were destroyed. The entire population, except the very poorest, were taken into captivity in Babylon. Seventy years passed before a handful of the people (primarily the priests and their families) were allowed to return home. Under the leadership of Nehemiah, they rebuilt the walls of Jerusalem, and a smaller version of the Temple Solomon had originally built.

"So by this time, the time of Jesus, more than 500 years later, there is still a lot of tension between Judah from the south and Galilee from the north. The southern Jews think those in Galilee have intermarried with Gentiles and become impure. Those in the north think Judeans are snobs. Yet, even though the Judeans are of purer blood and are more orthodox in the practice of their faith, Jesus, as you have seen, seems to have a special attraction to the north. After all, it was home. He was brought up in Galilee, performed his first miracle there, chose his disciples from that region, and he will preach his first sermon in a synagogue at Nazareth in Galilee."

"And," Mr. Pilgrim added, "he's on his way back there right now. How come?"

"I'm not completely sure," Jesna responded. And she truly did look puzzled.

"Maybe he feels that it is a darker place and needs more of the light of his presence. Maybe the people there are simply more open to his 'good news' than the more self-satisfied and privileged of Judea."

"Or," Pete volunteered, "maybe he just likes his momma's cooking."

Mr. Pilgrim and Jesna exchanged a long look. It was hard to argue with a theologian like Pete.

FAMILY DISCUSSION

1. Why to you think God arranged for his Son to be brought up among the outcasts?

2. Have you ever felt like an outsider?

3. Why do you think it might be easier for an outcast to enter God's kingdom than it would be for someone who is part of the "in" crowd?

SCENE THIRTY-ONE
THE WOMAN AT THE WELL[50]

As we traveled, Jesna continued her history and geography lessons. She explained to us that to get from Judea to Galilee you had to travel north and pass through Samaria. Samaria is in the heart of the land that used to be the home of the ten northern tribes of Israel—the "lost tribes." As Jesna spoke, the sun kept climbing up to its highest point in a clear-blue, Samaritan sky. It began to beam down heat rays that could melt a cactus.

The heat was causing everyone's clothes to stick to their skin like tape and their hair to clump together in thick, drop-dripping strands. I was panting.

Jesus and his disciples, with their sweaty, matted hair and mottled robes, made their way to a large pile of round stones and collapsed beside them. The stones looked like a giant pile of bread loaves a bakery had discarded. Scraggly shade from two would-be trees spread out across Jesus and his friends like tiny dark clouds.

"Psst, Jesna, why don't you turn on the air-conditioning?"

"Sorry, Pete. You want to feel the same things they do, don't you?"

As Pete was shaking his head 'no,' Jesus began to tell his disciples about the stone pile. He explained that the stones came from the upper walls of the very same well Jacob had dug many centuries ago. The same well that kept his twelve sons alive—the sons that had become the fathers of the twelve tribes of Israel.

The eyes of the disciples got wider. They were obviously impressed that Jesus seemed to know the history of every rock on the planet. I don't think it had sunk in yet that he had made each one.

After they rested, one of the disciples volunteered the group to go into the nearby town, Sychar, to buy some food for lunch. The same disciple suggested that Jesus wait by the well in a patch of shade.

"Bring me a cherry Icee," Pete shouted to their backs as they were leaving.

Long after the disciples left, a woman approached the well to draw water. Just after she had hoisted the first of her clay buckets from the well, Jesus asked her if she would give him a drink.

The woman looked at Jesus as if his face were green. She sat the pot of water on the ground and said:

"Are you, a Jew, asking me, a Samaritan woman, for a drink?"

Jesna saw our puzzled looks and quickly explained that Jews in those days would not be caught dead talking to a Samaritan. They viewed them as different, and very inferior.

Jesus answered, "If you knew the generosity of God and who I am, you would be asking *me* for a drink, and I would give you fresh, living water."

The woman, who seemed to have the spunk of a terrier pup, yelped back:

"Sir, you don't even have a bucket.... So how are you going to get this 'living water'? Are you a better man than our ancestor Jacob, who dug this well?..."

Jesus said, "Anyone who drinks the water I give will never thirst—not ever. The water I give will be an artesian spring . . . gushing fountains of endless life."

"Sir, give me this water..."

He said, "Go call your husband and then come back."

"I have no husband."

"That's nicely put: 'I have no husband.' You've had five husbands, and the man you're living with isn't even your husband."

"Whoa!" said Pete, "This is getting better than a soap opera!"

All the color that could escape the woman's sun-darkened face drained out. She finally stammered:

"Oh, so you're a prophet. Well, tell me this: You Jews insist that Jerusalem is the only place for worship, right? Our ancestors worshiped God at this mountain."

"Believe me, woman, the time is coming when you Samaritans will worship the Father neither here at this mountain nor there in Jerusalem.... It's who you are and the way you live that count before God.... That's the kind of people the Father is out looking for: those who are simply and honestly *themselves* before him in their worship. God is... Spirit. Those who worship him must do it out of their very being, their spirits, their true selves, in adoration."

The Samaritan woman's eyes were flashing puzzlement and intrigue. Her mouth flashed a reply:

"I don't know about that. I do know that the Messiah is coming. When he arrives, we'll get the whole story."

Jesus looked at her with beams of kindness that could melt a cactus-heart.

"I am he," said Jesus. "You don't have to wait any longer or look any further."[51]

Just at that moment the disciples returned. Their shocked expressions were bouncing off their knees as they walked.

"What's wrong with them?" Priscilla asked. "They look like they've seen a ghost."

"They can't believe Jesus was talking to a Samaritan woman," Jesna said. "They would probably have been less surprised if he had been talking to a cat that had mange." Oooo. I saw her point.

As Jesna spoke, the woman took the hint that was being silently blared at her by the disciples and left. But she walked away with lighter steps than the ones that had brought her to the well—she hardly moved any sand at all.

Jesna turned to us and explained, "These friends of Jesus still have a lot to learn about their teacher. The richest man in the universe goes out of his way to find the poor and diseased, the fishermen and tax collectors, the outcasts of society."

She continued, "The word Samaria means 'watch tower,' you know. And from it Jesus can see the hard, rocky ground that is the hearts of the Pharisees, and the rich fertile soil that is the hearts of the outcasts. You can bet he will do his best to draw up living water from Jacob's new well to irrigate both dry fields."

FAMILY DISCUSSION

1. What do you think Jesus meant by "living water"?

2. How do you think the woman felt when Jesus dared to speak to her? What did she feel when the disciples showed their displeasure?

3. Do you know an "outcast" that you can make feel better by being friendly tomorrow?

SCENE THIRTY-TWO
JESUS' PREACHING AT NAZARETH[52]

We hung around with Jesus and the disciples without doing any button-pushing time-leaps. Many of the people from the village of Sychar believed the story the Samaritan woman told them—that the Messiah was wearing a sweaty robe and sitting by Jacob's well. Somehow it seemed right that that's where a Messiah would be. They came out, first in trickles, and then in gully-washers of outcast humanity.

When the crowd asked Jesus to stay with them, he agreed, even though the disciples recoiled. So we spent the next two days with the Samaritans of Sychar; but not by Jacob's well. It seemed that each person in town was excited to have Jesus and his disciples come to his or her home. They wanted to treat him as much like royalty as their meager cupboards would allow.

By the time Jesus said he must leave, the disciples had all taken off their "better-than-thou" masks and were looking at the Samaritans like they were people with skin and hearts, instead of like diseased cats. Jesus seemed really pleased. The last few hours in Samaria he appeared to take turns smiling first at Samaritans and then at the disciples.

From the town of Jacob's well we went north. After a one day ride and a night under the stars, the rolling hills of Jesus' boyhood home, Nazareth, were once again in view and then under our feet.

As we walked the dusty streets, which seemed unusually quiet in the soft sunlight of early evening, Pete said, "Hey, isn't there going to be a band playing or something? What kind of welcome is this for a hometown hero?"

"No bands today, Pete," Jesna answered. "It's the Sabbath, God's day, and everybody is trying to be quiet and reverent. Plus, nobody in town except Joseph, Mary, and maybe a disciple or two know that the 'carpenter's son' is the Universe-Builder's boy."

"Yeah," Pete added, "and I bet the tuba hasn't even been invented yet."

Jesus led his small band to the front porch of a building made of stone—just one lick told me it was limestone—that wasn't much bigger than the Pilgrims' two-story home.

We followed a small crowd of people inside and I hopped up beside everybody else on a long wooden bench on the back wall.

"I wonder if Jesus made this bench," Pete mused.

"Could have," Jesna returned, with her forehead crinkled in thought.

After a few moments she whispered, "This is a synagogue. It's a Jewish church building. Almost every community has one. The size depends on how many people live there, and how generous they are. The Jewish people started building synagogues during their captivity by the Babylonians. It was a sort of Temple substitute."

"Sorta a 'temple-lite'?"

"You could say that, Pete," Jesna was getting used to Pete's strange remarks.

There wasn't much inside the stone church. The place was pretty dark and the only two windows didn't seem to be trying very hard to let the light in. I admit, it was hard for me to see.

I could see that there was a large wooden structure that looked like an unpainted, backyard gazebo. It was at the front of the room. Wooden benches, divided by a center walkway, ran from the front door of the synagogue to the base of the wooden structure. And, there was a large, wooden, upright chest, standing at attention next to the gazebo.

I noticed that the men were sitting on one side of the church and the women on the other. I also noticed that the people in the front of the building seemed to be dressed in finer and cleaner clothes than those in the back.

Jesus was sitting way at the back, just in front of Mr. Pilgrim. He was rocking back and forth, just slightly, with his lips moving in silent prayer. There was a shiny glaze of perspiration on his forehead. I wondered if he were feeling well.

In a few minutes an old man with a bald head and curly grey beard that sprawled out in three or four directions, stood up and walked over to the gazebo and stepped up inside. He turned and faced the congregation.

He led them in a group prayer. The words, "Hear, O Israel,

the Lord our God, the Lord is One, and thou shalt love the Lord thy God with all thy heart, and with all thy soul, and with all thy might."

He talked more. The audience talked back in response.

"Psst, hey Dad, when are they going to play the organ?"

"Do you see an organ, little brother?" Priscilla whispered sarcastically.

"Are you a dad?" Pete shot back.

Mr. Pilgrim whispered a "Shhh," then pulled Pete onto his lap for a better view. Pete seemed to like that.

After a while the man in charge pointed into the congregation. Mr. Pilgrim gulped so hard his Adam's apple tapped Pete on the back of the head, twice. "I think he's pointing at you, Dad. He wants you to come down front." They had both forgotten no one could see them.

But before Mr. Pilgrim could manage to sink any lower, Jesus slowly stood to his feet and walked down the center aisle.

As he made his way, the older man walked over to the large wooden chest, opened its doors and carefully pulled out two sticks which were encircled by thick paper. He handed them to Jesus who received the gift as one would a newborn baby. Then he turned to walk up the two steps of the gazebo.

"Mary and Joseph must be proud," the man beside me whispered. "That's their boy, Jesus, you know? He and his father made most of the furniture in here."

Pete's head did an "I knew it" nod, and then said to them, "And he and his other Father made you."

"Nobody can hear you, little brother," Priscilla reminded him.

"Oh."

Jesus was facing the crowd. The sun, now on Sabbatical itself, was giving no light. His face was well lit, though, by two large candles. He looked very serious and serene, as he let his eyes find every other pair in the room. An uncomfortable amount of time passed before he began slowly to unroll the scroll. He found his place and then read the most important words that ever passed from eye to tongue:

"God's spirit is on me;
he's chosen me to preach the Message of good
news to the poor,
Sent me to announce pardon to prisoners and
recovery of sight to the blind,
To set the burdened and battered free,
to announce, 'this is God's year to act!'"[53]

He rolled up the scroll and handed it back to the bearded man, who received it with hands trembling so hard that he almost dropped it.

A familiar voice whispered, "I don't like the way he kept emphasizing the word 'me.' It was almost as if..."

Then Jesus spoke in a loud, sure voice, "Today this Scripture has been fulfilled in your hearing!" Then he bowed his head as the crowd began to buzz like a swarm of angry bees. The Pilgrims exchanged worried looks with each other and then with Jesus. It was obvious he was about to get stung.

FAMILY DISCUSSION

1. Why do you think Jesus received a better reception from the Samaritans than he did from the people in his hometown?

2. How do you think Jesus felt as he was announcing to the people who had seen him grow up that he was their long-awaited Savior?

3. If you were one of his disciples, what would you be thinking about doing when Jesus finished reading?

SCENE THIRTY-THREE
MIRACULOUS ESCAPE[54]

"Hey!" someone from the crowd shouted, "You're Joseph's son. What do you think we are? Imbeciles? We've all known you since you were a kid."

Then from another corner of the church, "A donkey must have kicked you in the head while you were in Jerusalem. Go back to your seat before God sends a thunderbolt to shut you up!"

Jesus raised his hands to quiet the crowd. It didn't work. So, he raised his strong voice to speak louder than the angry swarm of noise.

"I know that a prophet is not accepted in his hometown," he said.

"But you're no prophet!" returned the quick echo.

Jesus continued, "Isn't it a fact that there were many widows in Israel at the time of the prophet Elijah, during the three and a half years of drought and famine? However, the only one to whom Elijah was sent didn't live in Israel, but Sidon. She was the one who received him as a prophet."

"Yeah, well why don't you leave here and go find a widow to tell that you are God's Son? But don't do it in this sacred place. Don't do it where we can hear you."

Jesus continued in a louder voice, "And weren't there many lepers in Israel at the time of the prophet Elisha, but the only one cleansed was Naaman," (and he paused for emphasis) "the Syrian?"

At that point it was as if Jesus' words kicked over the beehive. A buzzing storm, wearing sandals and bathrobes, swept into the aisles of the synagogue and down to the front. They seized Jesus, pulled him down from the wooden pulpit and pushed him out of the building and into the dusty streets—the same streets where Jesus had laughed and played as a boy.

Pete was in tears. He looked like he was watching a horror movie. "Do something, Dad! They look so angry I think they'll kill him."

Jesna put a soft hand on Pete's arm and Mr. Pilgrim said, "I don't know what to do, Pete. If I hit one of them they wouldn't even feel it."

"But," Pete sobbed, "at least Jesus would know we were trying to help."

Jesna moved her hand from Pete's arm to his shoulder and said, "He knows you want to help, Pete. He knows."

"How can he?" Pete snapped back.

The bee swarm took the shape of a lynch mob. While the Pilgrims, Jesna, and the disciples followed behind, I raced ahead to see what was going to happen to Jesus.

Oh no! From out in front I could see where the mob was heading—to a cliff at the edge of the village. As they marched, people in the crowd took turns stinging Jesus with their words. "Don't you ever come back to this town, blasphemer!"

"Anyone that would say what you said is the son of the Devil, not God."

"We'll make sure you never come back, unless you figure out a way to come back from the dead."

The crowd stopped at the edge of the cliff. Two strong-armed men held Jesus' arms behind his back, so close to the rocky edge that there was nothing under his toes but sixty feet of air, and if he went over, death.

"Throw him over!"

"It's what God would want!"

"You heard him blaspheme the name of the Holy One."

"Do it."

None of them could hear Pete hollering, "No!" And no one could believe what they saw next. Jesus left the strong men holding four handfuls of warm, night air as he slowly turned and walked back through the crowd as if he were strolling through a garden, as if they were a patch of wild flowers. He walked through their midst, and their middles, without disturbing a tassel on a robe—the same way we had passed through people in our car.

The mob became as quiet as church mice on padded pews; and they looked, of course, like they were seeing a ghost. After he had passed through the back row of "flowers," he walked over to the Pilgrims, who were standing with their mouths hanging open. Jesus patted Pete on the head with a solid, fleshy hand and said, "Thanks for being concerned about me."

"Oh, uh, you bet, Jesus. I thought you were a goner for a minute there." Jesus smiled, and after another head-pat, turned and walked toward his band of gaping disciples.

But before he could get there, Pete spoke up, "Hey, Jesus, could you teach me how to do that?"

Jesus turned back to face him and let out a hearty laugh.

"Now, Pete, don't you think that would be a little unfair to the other football players?" And he rejoined his team.

FAMILY DISCUSSION

1. What do you think the Pilgrims were thinking when the crowd of Jesus' friends and neighbors became a murdering mob?

2. What were you feeling when they were about to throw Jesus over the cliff?

3. Jesus can do the impossible. Do you have something impossible or difficult that he can help you work out?

SCENE THIRTY-FOUR
THE HEALING OF THE DEMONIAC IN THE SYNAGOGUE[55]

"Come on," Jesna said. "Let's get in the car. Jesus is heading down to Capernaum."

"But Jesna?"

"Yes, Priscilla."

"Won't the mob catch up with Jesus?…"

"And kill him?" Pete interrupted.

"Take a look. What do you think?" I looked and saw a whole synagogue-load of people slowly walking in as many different directions as there were noses. Most were scratching their heads—like a cat without a flea collar—and staring at the ground.

If there had been a cartoon caption drawn over the group, I imagine that it would read, "Oh my! I almost threw God over a cliff. I think I'll go home and fast for a few months."

"I see your point, Jesna," Priscilla said. With that we followed our own noses back to our car, which we had abandoned just outside the synagogue. Within minutes we had fallen in line behind Jesus and his band of friends.

The trip from Nazareth to Capernaum is both "up" and "down." It's "up" the face of a compass (from south to north) and "down" the mountains to the shore of the Sea of Galilee.

The view of the shimmering blue face of the Sea of Galilee from the green mountain slopes that tumble down into it can be breathtaking—and it takes a lot of beauty to take a dog's breath. We arrived in the fishing village that Jesus loved.

When the Sabbath came, we once again found ourselves with Jesus and his disciples in a synagogue. Jesus was in the middle of the stone church teaching a small circle of people. The people were very receptive to his teaching. Several complimented his wisdom, and one said:

"Rabbi, your teaching is so forthright, so confident and authoritative. You do not quibble and quote like the religion scholars we are used to hearing."

Jesus smiled at the one who had handed him the compliment, but said nothing. He didn't have time. For at that moment a man made an angry and frantic entrance into the room. He stopped, hovering over Jesus, who sat calmly on the stone floor.

In a deep, garbled voice, a voice that would've sounded more at home in the throat of a wolf, the man cried out:

"What business do you have here with us, Jesus? Nazarene! I know what you're up to! You're the Holy One of God and you've come to destroy us!"[56]

The raging man looked like a rabid animal. Saliva overflowed the boundaries of his lips and ran down his chin in two glistening streams. His eyes, dark and cold, flashed bright beams of rage. Ragged clothes covered small sections of his wiry body. Filth covered the rest.

The students of Jesus were tumbling over themselves trying to get out of harm's way. Jesus had not moved. Then, he moved his chin up a few inches and met the flames of anger that burned out of the animal-man's eyes with two deep pools of compassion.

Then Jesus spoke in a quiet but authoritative voice, "Be silent and come out of him!"

Instantly the man began to convulse, as if he were having a seizure. Then, it was as if he were pushed to the ground by the unseen hand of a giant. The man lay uninjured on the floor. His breathing was slow and calm. The thing was gone that had been tormenting him and causing him to act like an animal. Someone finally said:

"What's going on here? Someone whose words make things happen? Someone who orders demonic spirits to get out and they go?"[57]

"Wow!" said Priscilla as she was punching the buttons on her wrist computer. "What was that?"

"I don't know," said Pete, his voice out-shaking his hands. "It looked like something from a Stephen King movie. I hope it's going to be a long intermission."

"You can save your fingertips, Priscilla. I can tell you what that was. It was one of Satan's jaded miracles—an earthen pot in which he has turned the water into sewage. The pot's empty now, though." She motioned with her head to where Jesus sat on the floor, the head of the sleeping animal-man in his lap. "But I'm sure Jesus will fill it back up, with new wine, if the now empty man will give him half a chance."

FAMILY DISCUSSION

1. Why do you think Jesus was able to remain so calm when everyone else was so frightened?

2. How do you think the man felt after the demon was made to leave?

3. How would you act differently tomorrow if Jesus were to take away your pain or fears, and let you rest with your head in his lap?

SCENE TWENTY-FIVE
THE HEALING OF PETER'S MOTHER-IN-LAW[58]

The man's head was still in Jesus' lap as the disciples and his other pupils came from their hiding places under benches and behind stone columns. Slowly they settled in the circle around Jesus.

A man from the crowd, passing by Jesus, stooped and draped his own coat over the man who was using Jesus' lap for a pillow. He even tucked it in a little. This brought a smile to three faces— one dirty, one clean, one holy.

After about one Bible-hour had passed, the man who was now empty on the inside got up and took a seat in the circle. He sat there drinking in the words of Jesus.

After a while, Jesus stood to leave. As he walked and talked his way out of the synagogue, the small crowd of learners became a moving circle around him. They went out into the Sabbath-quiet Capernaum streets, and slowly went their separate ways.

Jesus was alone with his disciples when a little boy not much older than Pete came running up to Simon Peter. He began to tug on Simon's robe (which still smelled of fish) and he said in an anxious voice, "You've got to go home. They've sent me for you. Your mother-in-law is burning up with a fever. It won't go back down."

Simon looked at Jesus with anxious, questioning eyes. After receiving a nod in return he broke into a jog. Andrew caught up with him and matched his pace, stride-for-stride.

Jesus followed the four pairs of sand-spraying sandals, at a much slower tempo. We followed just behind the slower paced group Jesus was leading.

"This ought to be real interesting," we heard one disciple say to another.

"What did he mean, Jesna? Is Simon Peter's mom going to die?"

"No, Pete, no one is going to die. And, it's his mother-in-law, not his mother, who is sick. You see, the mother of Simon Peter's wife hasn't spoken to him since he left his boat bobbing in the Sea of Galilee to follow Jesus."

"My goodness!" exclaimed Pete, "Doesn't she know who Jesus is? I mean, you'd think she would be real happy that her son-in-law is working for God now."

"But she doesn't know that Jesus is God, little brother," Priscilla interrupted. "She must think her son-in-law has lost his mind, or something. I mean, he is sort of out of control."

"You're exactly right, Priscilla. Peter is 'out of control.' Being a fisherman isn't the highest paying job in Capernaum to begin with. She'd already written off the notion of her daughter having anything other than a meager living—from hook to mouth.

"Then, all of a sudden, Peter leaves his boat floating in the water, untied and on board was the biggest haul of fish he had ever caught to go and follow an even poorer man around as he wanders the countryside. He even gave all the fish—a good week's wages—away!"

"Oh. I see your point, Jesna," Mrs. Pilgrim said, as she reached over and ran her fingers through Priscilla's hair.

At that moment we found ourselves following Jesus through the narrow doorway of a small stone house. We followed him past an open fireplace and around a few pieces of rough-hewn furniture to a straw bed against the back wall of the house.

On the bed lay an old woman. Her coarse hair was a weathered forest of black and white. Her skin was dark from the sun. A film of sweat sat on top of a dry and cracked landscape, like soda on a Stainmaster carpet. In the thin light that came from a window high over her bed, we could see that it would be a closer walk for her to death than back to life.

Jesus stood over the woman and met her eyes with a calm smile. Then, with a clear voice he told the fever to leave. The woman's body gave a quick flinch and she sucked in a small gasp of air. No one thought to say goodbye as her fever left the room.

Jesus bent down and gave the woman a kiss on the forehead, turned away and began to leave. But before he made it to the doorway, Peter's mother-in-law was out of bed and on her feet.

"Wait!" she said, "You'll all be staying for dinner, won't you?"

The disciples exchanged puzzled looks.

"You have to stay. I can't have Simon Peter doing God's work on an empty stomach. He's my only son-in-law, you know."

They stayed to dinner and we stayed to watch.

FAMILY DISCUSSION

1. How do you think Simon Peter's mother-in-law felt about his giving up his job to follow Jesus?

2. What do you think she felt when she realized Simon Peter's new Boss could boss fevers around?

3. Why do you suppose she was so quick to do something nice for Jesus and his friends?

SCENE THIRTY-SIX
THE SICK HEALED AT EVENING[59]

"Go! Shoo! All of you. Out to the porch, I've got work to do in here." Simon Peter's mother-in-law said this while flapping her robe at Jesus and the disciples as if they were a flock of geese.

The crowd tumbled out onto a stone porch that was covered by a canopy of cloth. Peter became the centerpiece of a group back-patting activity.

"I guess 'high-fives' haven't caught on yet," Pete said. "I wish they could see me, I could show them how it's done." He then grabbed his sister by the elbow and held it so that her palm was over his head. Then he proceeded to slap at her hand while saying, "Psst! Jesus. Look over here. Get 'em to do this. It'll catch on."

Priscilla ended the celebration lesson by jerking her hand away and giving Pete's knee a low-five with her foot.

Jesus and the disciples settled into a relaxed late-afternoon conversation in such a natural manner that it made me think of Andy Griffith and his front porch in Mayberry. A guitar and a pitcher of lemonade would have fit well in the scene.

It wasn't long before chopping, stirring, and dough-flopping noises came outside the house and joined us on the porch. The sounds were soon followed by the smells of wheat, barley, lentils, cucumbers, cumin, mint, onions, figs, dates, and garlic. From all the different aromas it became obvious to all that it was not a meal, but a feast that was being prepared.

"I'm going to hide under the table and ask Jesus for some of his leftovers," Pete announced. *That's not a bad idea,* I thought to myself. *I'll join him.*

Jesna interrupted both of our daydreams. "Pete, I know it's hard to believe, but you're only about fifty-five seconds hungrier than when we left Daffy World."

When the feast was completed, Jesus and his friends were welcomed back into the house. They reclined on their sides, on the stone floor, around three sides of a low-lying table. The side closest to the fireplace was kept open so that Simon Peter's wife and mother-in-law could have free passage to serve the guests.

The meal was eaten from clay plates. And, they ate in a way that I am accustomed to—without silverware or chop sticks. However, they didn't eat with their faces or growl at each other. They used their fingers and torn pieces of bread as silverware to carry food to their mouths, and only their stomachs growled.

After the meal the well-fed group thanked their hostess and returned to the front porch. Well, at least they tried to.

Jesus walked out from the house of the fisherman's family into a sea of humanity. It seemed that the whole city had washed up in the front yard.

Jesna explained that the cleansing of the man possessed by a demon had caused word of Jesus to quickly spread throughout Capernaum. It was only politeness that had kept the crowd from interrupting his supper.

Jesus did not seem surprised by the gathering. He surveyed the faces and then waded out into the midst of twisted limbs, tree-branch crutches, dirty bandages, bleeding sores, burning foreheads, and every kind of suffering imaginable.

As he went through the crowd, he stopped and looked gently into each pair of expectant eyes. Sometimes he would say nothing and simply reach out and touch the place of pain. Sometimes he would touch and speak. Every time he left wholeness where there had been a hole.

Occasionally, he would come face to face with someone with wild, darting eyes, men with demons like the man he had healed in the synagogue. More than once, after praying for one of these men, their eyes would become clear and then a shrieking voice— no longer coming from the body to which it had been attached— would scream out, high above the crowd, "You are the Son of God!"

But he shut them up each time; refusing to let them say more. No sound, other than a whimper, followed his rebuke.

The hour was very late when Jesus had prayed for the last remnant of the crowd and retired to a spot on the floor of Simon Peter's house to sleep.

Before Jesus went to sleep, Pete yawned out a question for Jesna. "Why did Jesus make the demons be quiet? You'd think he would want everybody to know who he really is."

"Pete," Jesna said back to a pair of half-closed eyelids, "There are probably a couple of reasons. First, if you had some really special news to tell someone, would you want to tell them your-self, or have your worst enemy do it?

"But, I think there is a more important reason," she went on. "Being the Messiah isn't just about power and miracles. It's also about suffering. Jesus doesn't want to tell everything about who he is until people see the whole story including the way he will die."

Pete's face was very serious. Apparently he didn't know what to think about a God who would choose to die.

FAMILY DISCUSSION

1. What do you think about Jesna's answer to Pete?

2. What do you think it felt like to see Jesus use touch and words to untwist a twisted limb?

3. How do you think the people who were healed lived their lives differently the next day?

SCENE THIRTY-SEVEN
JESUS DEPARTS FROM CAPERNAUM[60]

"Ouch! Hey, who stepped on my hair?"

"Sorry, Sis. But you really shouldn't be putting your hair where people can put their feet. Besides, Jesna said it's time to get up."

"What time is it?" Mr. Pilgrim said just before a yawn took control of his mouth.

"It's 4:00 A.M., Bible time." Priscilla answered, then said, "Hey, what's going on here?"

"Jesus is already up and on his way," Jesna said. "We've got to get going if we're going to catch up with him."

"Where's he going this time of the night—to raid the refrigerator? His disciples are still cutting Zs over there."

"He often gets up this early, Pete. It's his habit to go out before the sun comes up, to a quiet place, to talk to his Father."

The Pilgrim family slowly disentangled themselves from their brief night's sleep. I stretched first my front and then my back and then I shook all over. We all flopped into the car like a pack of tired zombies. Jesna punched a couple of buttons and we were in motion.

"Phewee," Pete said, "somebody's got dog breath."

"Not me," everyone said at once through tightly pinched lips. I was left to wonder what's so bad about having dog breath. Soon Capernaum was in our rearview mirror and we were out in the quiet countryside.

"Shhh!" Jesna said, even though no one was talking. "There's Jesus."

Straight ahead Jesus sat on the ground. He was using the trunk of an olive tree as a back rest. His eyes were closed and his robe was moving very slowly with his steady breathing.

"Did he go back to sleep?" Pete asked.

"No. He's not asleep. He's praying, talking to his Dad. This is how they stay in touch. This is the secret to Jesus' ministry— spending lots of quiet time listening to what his Father has to say, and asking questions."

We sat there close to Jesus for a couple of hours as he prayed in the soft, gray moonlight. Sometimes his lips would move. Sometimes a smile would break across his face. And one time, a tear slid down his cheek. He was a picture of tranquility, and of deep emotion.

A pink and orange dawn came and awoke the green, blue, and brown colors of the landscape.

"Jesus!" someone shouted. "Jesus, where are you?" another, more anxious voice asked. The noise brought Jesus' eyes back to life. The crunching sounds of sandals on sand and dry grass, caused him to turn his head and see his band of disciples approaching.

"Where have you been?" Simon Peter asked. "Everybody's looking for you. After what happened last night, word has gotten around. You've got to go back. There's work to be done."

"Yes," Jesus said, "there is much work to be done. But, we'll be going on to the rest of the villages so I can preach there also. This is why I have come."

"You mean," Simon said, "we're not going back to where the crowd has gathered?"

"Not now," was all Jesus said in return.

We followed along as a determined Jesus led his doubtful friends along the shore of the Sea of Galilee, away from a guaranteed revival. We headed to travel the unknown.

"Jesna."

"Yes, Priscilla."

"Why isn't Jesus going back to Capernaum? Why is he going on to another town?"

"You'll have to ask his Father that. Jesus is just obeying what he heard from his Dad this morning. Taking the time to listen and being willing to obey is the secret to the ministry of Jesus, and it's the way we are able to live in his Father's kingdom. Listening to God can cause us to march to the beat of a different drummer."

FAMILY DISCUSSION

1. Do you think it is possible to actually "hear" from God when you pray?

2. How does it feel when he speaks to you?

3. Why don't you take a moment and ask him a question right now, like, "What do you think about me?" or, "What is one thing you would like for me to do tomorrow?"

SCENE THIRTY-EIGHT
THE CLEANSING OF THE LEPER[61]

We followed Jesus and his disciples as they went to villages throughout Galilee.

He always began by going to the town's synagogue. There he would take a seat and begin teaching. He always taught about the "kingdom of God."

What he said was simple, but brimming full of stories, pictures, and parables.

In no time at all a crowd would gather around him—just like when he was a twelve-year-old boy and the centerpiece of the Temple in Jerusalem. The crowd would join him on the ground and then become very still and quiet.

When he would finish speaking there would be questions, and there would be people marveling at the way he spoke with such certainty and with such authority.

I heard one person say, "It's almost as if he knows God personally, the way he speaks for him."

"Shhhh! Don't say that!" was the shocked response. "Do you want to be struck dead for blaspheming?"

It was obvious that most people did not yet understand Jesus or his Father.

One day after Jesus had finished teaching about his Dad's kingdom and the rules for living there, we left the synagogue and got back on the road to the next town.

Not very long after stepping back into the countryside, one of the disciples looked behind us and gasped, "Oh no! A leper is following us! Let's run for it!"

This caused all the Pilgrims and me to immediately turn our faces in the opposite direction from which their feet were still pointing. "Did he say a leopard is following us?" Pete almost yelled. Then he looked at me and said, "Get 'em, girl!"

"Not a leopard, Pete," Priscilla said, "a leper." But by this time Pete had sized up the situation.

"Hey, there ain't no leopard behind us. It's just somebody wrapped up like a mummy." I breathed a sigh of relief.

A mummy? I thought. My relief was short-lived.

Jesus stopped and turned to face the stranger. His disciples fell in line behind him, braced to run, just like a lineup of Olympic sprinters awaiting the start gun.

Jesus began to walk toward the stranger. The disciples inched away, in the opposite direction, listening for the signal to begin the race.

The man draped in strips of dirty cloth stopped in his tracks and said, "No, don't come close to me. I'm unclean."

Jesus didn't stop. He walked toward the man with his hand outstretched. "No!" a disciple shouted. "You can't touch him or you'll die, too."

At that moment the wind blew back part of the dirty wrapper from the man's face, exposing it to the sunlight and a host of disbelieving eyes.

The sudden sight of his face caused all four Pilgrims to suck in huge gasps of air. If a dog were ever to shriek, it would have been me, just then.

The sick man's face was covered with brownish-red spots. Sitting on top of these were thick clusters of dark nodules, and running sores. It was hard to tell, for sure, that the mass of decay we saw had ever actually been a face—two dark, hope-filled eyes were the only clue to what it had once been.

The leper dropped to his knees and cried out through what

had once been a mouth, "Jesus, if you want to, you can make me clean."

Jesus looked at the man and then back at his disciples. His eyes had become pools of tears. He then took a couple more steps toward the man and, as several disciples cried, "No!" he touched him and said, "I do want to. Be clean."

At first the man pulled away from the touch, as if he didn't want to scald Jesus' hand with his face. Then he stopped and nuzzled the holy hand between his chin and shoulder.

The sight sent tears steaming down four sets of Pilgrim's cheeks and one set of dog cheeks. Then Jesna really opened the floodgates when she said, "That's probably the first time he's been touched by another human being in a long time."

After a while Jesus moved his hand up the side of the man's face to the top of his head, brushing back the dirty rags as he did.

There, beaming out from the middle of a rag-heap, was the brand-new face of a handsome teenage boy. There wasn't even a zit to be seen anywhere on the peach-fuzzed landscape.

The young man must have caught sight of his new, old face, in the mirror of Jesus' eyes, because he grabbed it with two brand new hands and let out a scream that could have been heard above the noise of a football stadium full of roaring fans.

The former leper leapt to his feet, picked Jesus up by the waist, and danced him in a circle.

When he finally put Jesus' feet back on earth he began to dance again.

Before he could promenade back into town Jesus said:

"Say nothing to anyone. Take the offering for cleansing that Moses prescribed and present yourself to the priest. This will validate your healing to the people."[62]

But it was hard to tell if the young man had heard Jesus' words over the music playing in his head.

Jesus returned to his place at the front of the band of disciples and they continued their walk toward the next town. The disciples were giving him a little more space than before. It was hard to tell if it was for fear of contamination or respect for holiness.

"Well," Pete said with a sly grin. "I guess with Jesus, a leper really can change his spots." That was enough to make a dog groan. But there was no denying it, Jesus could clean a person up, inside or out.

FAMILY DISCUSSION

1. Do you know any diseases today, like leprosy, that people are deathly afraid they might catch?
2. How would you feel if you were abandoned and near death, like the leper, and then you were suddenly made clean and whole again?
3. What would you want to do for the One who had caused you to be clean from disease?... from sin?

SCENE THIRTY-NINE
THE HEALING OF THE PARALYTIC[63]

Apparently the cleansed leper was a pioneer in first-century mass communication. In spite of Jesus' request that he tell only the priest, news of the miracle spread faster than a plague.

The crowds around Jesus became much larger as they heard about his miracles. Soon he and the disciples began to keep to out-of-the-way places, because they could no longer move easily in the cities. But even in the obscure places, throngs of people found him.

After a few days of these larger crowds, Jesus returned to his home base of Capernaum. Within hours of his arrival the cat was out of the bag there, too. A huge crowd gathered around the doorway of the home where he was staying. They were wedged so tightly into the room where he sat that no one could get in or out or even close the door. A person would have needed a can of WD-40 to put a hand in his pocket.

Jesus did not complain. He just began to teach, as if the packed house was a synagogue on Sabbath morning.

"I wonder if anyone came here from Nazareth?" Pete said to Jesna with a wink.

His dad picked up on the humor and added, "I bet they think their hometown boy has done pretty good, now."

Jesna just smiled. She was probably glad the Pilgrims were paying such close attention.

Jesus was sitting by the hearth of an empty fireplace. People sat, stood, or reclined on an elbow, all around him. Their heads formed stair-steps from Jesus right to the back to the walls of the house. They looked like the crowd in a miniature football stadium.

A warm glow from the afternoon sun streamed in through two high square windows.

Then, all of a sudden, the light beams were alive with particles of dust and straw. "Ouch!" someone exclaimed as a good-sized chuck of splintered wood bounced from his head and into the lap of a neighbor.

"What's going on here?"

"Hey, somebody's trying to break in, through the roof."

"It's a little warm for Santa, isn't it?" Priscilla asked with a rare grin on her face.

"It may be, Prissy, but it sure sounds like a team of reindeer is prancing around up there."

At that moment a third rectangular beam of light suddenly exploded into the room... from above. And just behind the blast of outside light a man, strapped to boards, was lowered from above by strong arms.

The tightly wedged crowd somehow found a way to clear some space in the center of the room as a choir of "Ohs!" "Umphs!" and "Ouches!" began.

Jesus seemed impressed by the man's face. It was full of faith. From the awkward movements of his head and neck, and the lifelessness of his arms and legs, it was obvious that the man who owned the faith was a paraplegic.

The man looked up at Jesus and said only one word, "Please!" Jesus looked back at the man and said only, "Son, I forgive your sins."[64]

The man on the stretcher smiled a deep sigh. Jesus returned it.

But then, a cluster of black-robed men, who had taken the only stools in the house, stood to their feet and said in unison as they pointed at Jesus, "He can't talk that way! That's blasphemy! God and only God can forgive sins."

"Where have they been?" Pete said as he nudged Priscilla.

Jesus, who was now on his knees untying the limbs of the paraplegic, said as he worked:

"Why are you so skeptical? Which is simpler: to say to the paraplegic, 'I forgive your sins,' or say, 'Get up, take your stretcher, and start walking?'"[65]

Jesus then stood to his feet and waited for their answer. When none returned he said, as he looked at the black-robed men with intensity, "Well, just so it's clear that I'm the Son of God and authorized to do either, or both...."

He looked down at the paraplegic, who was still lying as motionless as a blown-over scarecrow, and said, "Get up. Pick up your stretcher and go home."

And, as dozens of gasps sucked the remaining scant supply of dirty air right out of the room, the man did just that. He stood up on wobbly legs like a newborn colt, bent over and picked up his stretcher, and walked out of the room; the crowd parted like the Red Sea before Moses.

Many in the crowd broke into applause. Many more rubbed their eyes in disbelief. The former paralytic clicked his heels together as he ran down the street. The black-robed men scowled as their faces turned the color of Rudolph's nose.

FAMILY DISCUSSION

1. Why do you suppose the black-robed men (Pharisees) became angry with Jesus when he told the paralytic his sins were forgiven?

2. Which do you think feels better, to have your sins forgiven, or to be healed of paralysis?

3. How do you think the former paralytic lived differently the next day?

SCENE FORTY
THE CALL OF LEVI (MATTHEW)[66]

A few moments after the crowd had seen a
scarecrow come to life and dance out the
door, Jesus stood to his feet and walked
outside. He went through the sea of
people who were still parted.

For some reason the crowd did
not follow him. Even his disciples
stayed some distance behind.

Jesus walked to the shore of the city of Capernaum—where the
stone and plaster buildings met the edge of the Sea of Galilee.

It was a picture-perfect day. The sun-bleached city stretched
out behind Jesus, up gentle slopes and rolling hills. The waters of
the Sea of Galilee were a bright turquoise blue and sparkled with
thousands of flashes of light.

"Look at all those twinkles on the water," Pete said. "It looks
like the fish are using flashbulbs to take pictures of Jesus."

Jesus turned and began walking along a wide street that followed the boundaries of the Sea of Galilee. The fish continued to
take their pictures. To his left was a long row of buildings. Since
there weren't any bread smells coming from any of them like
from the houses, I assumed we were in a business district.

After a while Jesus stopped. The disciples stopped, too, a few
spaces back, and we drove right through the middle of them.

"Pardon me," Mrs. Pilgrim said to the eleven holograms.

Jesus was staring at a man who sat outside one of the first-
century office buildings. He was dressed in bright, shiny clothes
and was huddled over a polished wooden table, scratching on
something. He looked very official. He must have been—to be

able to decide that the day was too pretty to work inside.

A long line of people stretched from the right of the man's table, back between buildings and out onto the street. It went about the length of four or five circus elephants standing trunk to tail.

Most of the faces of people in line looked troubled.

"What's wrong with those people, Dad? They look like their favorite team lost the Superbowl."

"I don't know, unless that man they're waiting to see works for the IRS."

"You are what, Dad?"

"IRS. The tax grabbers, Pete."

"You are very perceptive, Mr. Pilgrim. That man works for the Roman government that rules over this territory. He's a tax collector. Do you remember, Capernaum is one of the tax collecting stations for Rome? People around here, well, I guess throughout the Empire, hate tax collectors for several reasons. They remind the people that they are a conquered nation; they demand part of their hard-earned money; and most of them cheat. They demand more money than they are supposed to and put the extra in their own pockets...."

"Hey, Matthew!" Jesus' shout brought Jesna's lesson to an abrupt end. "Come on and go with me."

"He's talking to that IRS man isn't he?"

"Yep, sure is, Pete."

The man in the fine clothes looked up from his work to meet the eyes of Jesus. Then, without even taking the time to put a period at the end of a sentence, he stood up and walked down to where Jesus was standing by the Sea.

Jesus embraced the man and then the two continued walking.

Jesus had his arm around the former tax collector. The disciples followed, shaking their heads from side to side. They seemed more surprised to see this—Jesus turning a tax collector into a disciple—than when they heard about him turning water into wine.

Nightfall found Jesus and his disciples at Matthew's house enjoying a feast. One of the disciples called it Matthew's one-day-old birthday party.

Many of Matthew's friends were there. They were a smelly bunch. Not bad smells, exactly, but smells none the less. To my nose, his friends were a potpourri of wine, strong perfume, and incense. They sure knew how to laugh.

Matthew's house had a large front door and two oversized windows facing the sidewalk. All three were open that evening.

While most of the guests were enjoying third helpings, the celebration was interrupted by a blast from the sidewalk. Several black-robed men had been staring though one of the windows for several minutes. When one of them could be silent no longer he announced for all to hear—both inside and outside the house. "Why does your teacher eat with thieves and sinners?"

Jesus touched his embarrassed host on the arm, as if to say, "It's all right. I'll handle this." Then he said for all to hear:

"Who needs a doctor: the healthy or the sick? Go figure out what this Scripture means: 'I'm after mercy, not religion.' I'm here to invite outsiders, not coddle insiders."[67]

The lead black-robe, who had just lost his duel with Jesus, grabbed his robe and spun himself around. He marched off and the others followed. You could almost smell the smoke coming out of their ears as Jesus said to Matthew, "Happy birthday."

FAMILY DISCUSSION

1. What was Matthew willing to give up to follow Jesus? And, what were the Pharisees unwilling to give up?

2. How do you think the people standing in line to pay their taxes felt when Matthew quit his job?

3. How would a disciple's behavior likely be different from that of a Roman tax collector?

SCENE FORTY-ONE
THE QUESTION ABOUT FASTING[68]

The next morning, following the party at Matthew's house, Jesus and his disciples arose and left early. Matthew was with them. He was wearing the robe of a poor man and the smile of a king.

While they were still within view of Matthew's former home, they were approached by a group of men who smelled a lot like John the Baptist and who apparently were using his tailor to make their hairy clothes. Without so much as a greeting, one of the men spoke out:

"Why is it that we and the Pharisees rigorously discipline body and spirit by fasting, but your followers don't?"

"Those men are disciples of John the Baptist," Jesna whispered just before Jesus spoke:

"When you're celebrating a wedding, you don't skimp on the cake and wine. You feast. Later you may need to pull in your belt, but not now.... No one cuts up a fine silk scarf to patch old work clothes."

"Especially those camel hides they're wearing," Pete interrupted God to say.

"You want fabrics that match. And you don't put your wine in cracked bottles."[69]

When Jesus finished talking to them some of John's disciples were slowly nodding in agreement while others looked puzzled and glanced back and forth at each other, as if they were searching for an interpreter.

"Do you understand what Jesus is saying?" Jesna asked.

"No," Mr. Pilgrim said, with a "thanks for asking" tone in his voice.

"I think I do," Priscilla said.

"Tell us, please," Jesna encouraged.

"Well, Jesna, you told us that Jewish weddings are celebrations that last for seven days. They're lavish feasts with music and dancing, like nothing we can imagine today." Jesna's eyes were sparkling with anticipation as Priscilla continued. "Jesus is saying that time with him should be a celebration. After all, he is teaching about a whole new, happier way to live in his Father's kingdom. So, it's a time for joy, not sadness and self-denial."

"Yeah?" Pete interrupted. "Then why was he talking about wine and cracked pots, or something like that?"

Priscilla sucked her lips inside her mouth. After a few seconds passed she said, "I don't know." Pete looked more disappointed than satisfied that he had stumped his sister.

"May I help?" Jesna asked. Priscilla nodded yes.

"The Pharisees and the followers of John (to a much smaller extent) have 'old' ideas about God and about religion. It is their idea that you must sacrifice and deny yourself pleasure to find God.

"Jesus is bringing new ideas, 'new wine' that doesn't fit in their old religious system. He is saying that you first find God and experience joy (like that of a bride and groom at a wedding); then, being obedient and sacrificing will come more easily. But they'll need brand new containers to be able to hold what he is teaching."

We looked at what had been a united band of John's disciples. A few were still listening to Jesus. Listening and nodding. Others had already turned their backs to his new ideas and were walking away. You could almost see Jesus' new wine running out of their lives like it might from old, cracked earthen containers.

FAMILY DISCUSSION

1. What is the "new wine" that Jesus is talking about?

2. Describe the difference between obeying someone because you love him, and obeying him in hopes that he might love you.

SCENE FORTY-TWO
PLUCKING THE GRAIN ON THE SABBATH[70]

A few days after Jesus had been talking to John's disciples about "new wine," he and his disciples were on their way to a local synagogue. It was a crisp and clear Sabbath morning.

Along the way they passed a wheat field. The stalks of wheat were being turned into a rolling ocean by the gentle wind. Golden wave after golden wave came lapping in toward us. The sight of a rippling ocean in the midst of dry land was too much for the disciples to resist. They waded in.

Jesus stood by the roadside smiling, like a proud lifeguard. It was quite a sight, his twelve friends cavorting around waist-deep in waves of wheat.

The adventure was more than Pete and Priscilla could resist. "Last one in is a rotten egg," Pete announced to Priscilla. But it was he who dove in last.

After several minutes of running, jumping, cartwheeling, and grain surfing, Pete and Priscilla sat down in the middle of the field—becoming invisible to their parents who were still in the car with Jesna.

"Look at this stuff," Priscilla said, as she ran her finger alongside one of the wheat plants, from its base in the dry ground to its spindly tips. "Each stalk branches into seven, uh, limbs or ears, at the top. And each of the seven has dozens of grains. I wonder if there is something significant about God making each one with seven parts like this?"

"Huh?" Pete said. "I just wonder if you can eat it—it looks like breakfast on a stick."

"I guess you can," Priscilla said, a little impatiently. "Look over there."

We looked and saw Jesus' disciples. They had stopped swimming too, and were now pulling off the heads of grain and munching on them as if they were popcorn.

"Hum. Looks like a pretty dry breakfast," Pete said. "But, it's worth a try."

Pete forgot he was a hologram. But the wheat didn't.

His hand passed through a cluster of wheat grains as if he were a shadow.

"Shoooot!" he said.

"Hey! What are your disciples doing there?" an angry voice cried out. "They're breaking the Sabbath rules! Aren't you going to stop them, Jesus?"

Pete and Priscilla stood up so they could see over the wheat. I had to jump up real high (like I do when trying to catch a Frisbee) to see. It took a couple of jumps to get the full picture. Another group of black-robed men had encircled Jesus.

"Uh-oh," one of the disciples whispered. "We're in for it now."

But from the tone of Jesus' reply it seemed the only ones in for it were the Pharisees:

"Really?" Jesus was saying. "Didn't you ever read what David and his companions did when they were hungry, how they entered the sanctuary and ate fresh bread off the altar, bread that no one but priests were allowed to eat?

"…There is far more at stake here than religion. If you had any idea what this Scripture meant—'I prefer a flexible heart to an inflexible ritual'—you wouldn't be nitpicking like this."[71]

"Yeah," Pete blurted out, "Stop nitpicking the wheat picking."

The Pharisees didn't hear Pete; but they did hear Jesus. They turned away from him and continued their march to the synagogue. With their flushed faces they looked like a bundle of determined beets.

When Pete and Priscilla arrived back at the car, Jesna had a question waiting.

"Do you know what the bread that Jesus was referring to—the bread on the altar—is called?" She didn't wait for the answer she knew none of the Pilgrims had. "It's called the 'bread of the Presence,' and it symbolizes the presence of God in the sanctuary. That's what David and his friends ate."

She continued, after inspecting our faces for signs of understanding. "Those Pharisees were in the presence of the Son of God—the Bread of Life—and they were too angry and self-righteous to realize it."

"Oh well," Pete said. "You are what you eat."

FAMILY DISCUSSION

1. Do you think it was OK for the disciples to eat grain on the Sabbath?
2. What do you believe the disciples felt when Jesus was being criticized for what they were doing?
3. Have you noticed anything different about the way Pete and Priscilla have begun to behave in the past few scenes? What do you think has caused the change?

SCENE FORTY-THREE
THE MAN WITH THE WITHERED HAND[72]

We drove along behind Jesus and his disciples as they followed in the dusty footprints of the band of angry Pharisees. After a while I could see that their trail ended at the front door of a synagogue. I guess Pete could see it too. He said, "It looks like Jesus and those mean guys go to the same church. That would never happen where we live, would it?"

Mrs. Pilgrim smiled a slightly embarrassed smile and patted her son on the head.

"There's more going on in that building than 'church' this morning!" Jesna said. "The Pharisees have set a trap for Jesus. It's already baited."

"Huh?" all four Pilgrims said with one voice.

But it was too late for an explanation. Jesus was opening the door for his disciples. We crawled out of our time-car and followed them in.

He kept holding the door until Jesna, the Pilgrims, and all four of my feet were inside. "Thanks Mr. Jesus," Pete said as Jesus walked by us to take his place in front of his disciples. He patted Pete on the head.

It only took a couple of seconds to see that something wasn't right. It didn't take a dog's nose to sniff the rottenness in the air.

First of all, everybody in the synagogue was twisted in such a way that their knees were facing the front of the building while their faces were glued to Jesus, in the back. Also, the center aisle was a little wider than usual and, in the front of the room, surrounded by a semicircle of black-robed men, a man sat alone on the dirt floor.

While the man's face was merely dirty; his clothes were filthy. A long piece of cloth was wrapped around the top of his head as a turban.

When the man saw Jesus he held out both hands toward him like a toddler to its mother and grunted a pleading grunt. One of his hands, the right one, was withered and deformed.

"Is that poor man the bait?" Priscilla asked.

"Yes," Jesna replied, "but he doesn't know it. He just wants to be touched and healed."

"Well what's wrong with that?" Pete said. "If I had a hand like his, that's what I would want too!"

"It's the Sabbath, Pete. Religious law says that to heal on the Sabbath is breaking a rule. The Pharisees want to see if they can catch Jesus getting into trouble."

"Like eating breakfast in a wheat field?"

"Exactly, Pete."

"Whoa! I thought my parents were strict."

Jesus walked down the wide aisle and into the baited trap. But he didn't look like a frightened prey—he was walking more like a proud lion, out for a hunt.

When he reached the front of the room he stood behind the man with the crippled hand and faced the congregation. The pack of plotting Pharisees eagerly stepped backward to give him more room—to convict himself.

Then he spoke to the people:

"What kind of action suits the Sabbath best? Doing good or doing evil?" [He paused and let his eyes rest on the Pharisees, who stood close by, before returning his gaze to the congregation and continuing.] "Helping people or leaving them helpless?"[73]

No one said a word. Then Jesus looked back at the Pharisees. His eyes were flashing anger now, which was very unusual for *his* eyes. I had not seen anger there since he cleared the Temple in Jerusalem.

Pete must have seen it too. "Whooooeeee! Stand back folks. I think he's about to blow."

But the flash of anger quickly fizzled and sank into a pool of deep grief. The squirming Pharisees seemed more comfortable with his anger than this gaze of pity.

Jesus left the Pharisees in their confusion and turned his attention back to the man with the crippled hand. The man had spun around on the ground and was now facing Jesus.

Jesus took him by his hands and gently lifted him to his feet. Jesus said to the man, "Hold out your hand." He held it out and—it was as good as new. Better than new; it was also clean!

The crowd gasped.

The Pharisees, seeing the miracle God provided on this Sabbath, made a hasty exit out the mouth of their trap. It was obvious they were not pleased with the day's catch.

As they passed, I heard one grumble, "We'll have to get help from Herod if we're going to destroy him."

"Yeah. Well don't let the door hit you on the way out," Pete said.

"Shhh, little brother. Jesus has started to preach."

FAMILY DISCUSSION

1. What do you think was going through the minds of the people when they saw the withered hand made whole?

2. What do think the healed man will do with his new hand tomorrow?

3. If you were a disciple, you would know the Sabbath rules. How would you feel about Jesus' breaking the rules?

SCENE FORTY-FOUR
JESUS HEALS MULTITUDES BY THE SEA[74]

When the Sabbath day had ended, Jesus set off to take a special vacation with his friends. Jesna reminded us that he was not only fully God, but also fully man. The human part needed some rest; and the divine part had a big decision to make.

The thought of a vacation must have caused Priscilla to remember the one her family had been on—back at Daffy World. "Hey, look at my watch. Fifty-five earth-seconds have passed since we got on this ride. That only leaves five seconds." She sounded a little disappointed.

"I must say, Jesna," said Mrs. Pilgrim, "this is the best vacation we have ever had." That caused Jesna to smile and Mr. Pilgrim to give his wife a hug.

"Yeah, Mom, this is way more gooder than when Dad made us go in all those museums in Washington last summer."

"That's 'better,' not 'gooder,' Pete," said Mrs. Pilgrim.

"I know; I just keep forgetting. And it's ten times as good as when we marched around on all those battlefields where the Silver War was fought. Man, I'm sure glad there wasn't a ride like this at that place. We'd have been ducking bullets and dodging swords for years."

"That's Civil War, little brother, not Silver War. But I'm glad we didn't take a ride through that, too."

As the Pilgrims talked we continued to follow Jesus—deeper and deeper into the countryside of Galilee.

After a while we stopped. Jesus had selected a campsite, under a grove of olive trees, and within a Frisbee toss of the Sea of Galilee.

The shore was covered with an assortment of smooth, round, gray rocks. Some of the bigger ones would cause the sea waves to leap straight up into the air and turn into a thousand parachuting sparkles. I couldn't resist wading out to try and catch as many of them as I could with my mouth. Pete came in, too.

When nightfall came, a perfect vacation day got even better. Peter and Andrew, without any help from Jesus, had managed to catch a basketful of flapping fish. They were so proud. The evening was spent watching Jesus and his friends roast the catch by a large, open fire, and listening to them tell stories. Jesus could really make them laugh—us too.

After a while the Pilgrims began to tell their own tales. But it wasn't long until the disciples were sawing logs—sleeping. The Pilgrims and Jesna soon followed them into the lumber yard. We had a five-person and one-dog group snuggle by the fire.

The crowing of a distant rooster, early the next morning, brought an end to the night's sleep and to Jesus' vacation.

Before the sun was fully awake, the hills behind us came alive with trickles and then streams of people. Before breakfast Jesus was surrounded by two seas—Galilee on one side and sick and hurting humans on the other.

While the Sea of Galilee stayed calm, the sea to the west was a tempest that came crashing in on Jesus. People were desperate to make contact with his healing touch.

"These people are from all over," Jesna explained. "There are people here from down south, from Judea and from Jerusalem. Some have come from the other side of the Jordan and some from up north along the coast of the Mediterranean Sea."

"Wow!" Mr. Pilgrim said, sounding a little like Pete. "Word has really gotten out, hasn't it? And this is without any newspapers or TV."

"Or any CNN or kids' news magazines, either, Dad."

Word certainly had gotten out. The second day of Jesus' vacation was spent by his trying to swim through a tidal wave of broken people.

After many people were healed and many demons were sent packing, the crowd became even more excited and more expectant. They pushed in ever harder. At one point the human part of Jesus looked a little concerned, and he asked his disciples to get a boat ready in case they started getting trampled by the crowd.

But even so, it was obvious from the gentle smile on his face, and from his eyes which often welled with tears, that he enjoyed his work—even when it came on a vacation day.

FAMILY DISCUSSION

1. Were you surprised that Jesus would need a vacation?

2. What do you suppose it would feel like to sit with Jesus around a campfire, listening to stories and laughing?

3. Why do you suppose the hurting people were almost rude to Jesus and interrupted his vacation?

SCENE FORTY-FIVE
CHOOSING THE TWELVE[75]

When the afternoon was about half spent, Jesus gathered his band of friends together and told them that they would be heading up to the top of a mountain for the night. He instructed the crowd not to follow and said that he would return the next day.

Jesna assured us that it would be OK for us to continue tagging along, since no one but Jesus, angels, animals, and small children could see us. So we did.

Jesus led his followers up the rocky slope of a steep mountain. It was the same mountain by the sea that we had been standing on. By the time we got up to its summit everyone was exhausted.

Jesus sat down on a large rock at the peak of the highest ridge. Behind him was a green and brown backdrop of lesser mountains and rolling hills. Behind us was an aerial view of the Sea of Galilee, and the small ribbon of ant-sized people whom we had left below. Smoke from several campfires was making its way to heaven in lazy lines of brown and grey.

When Pete got a look at the crowd we had been with, just a few hours earlier, he said, "I wonder if that's how we look to God?"

Jesus, the only one who knew the answer to Pete's question, didn't respond. He seemed very serious and was surveying the faces of his friends. They sat before him on the ground in a semi-circle. Jesus had tears pooling at the bottoms of his eyes and a half-sad, half-joyful smile on his face.

"What's going on here?" Pete asked. "You could hear a feather drop."

"Jesus is about to pick the twelve friends who will be his closest disciples," Jesna answered. "He's sad because he won't be able to pick everyone here."

"So," Pete said, "this is sort of like when my baseball coach had to tell us who made the team and who didn't."

"Sort of like that, Pete, but different. He's not saying that only twelve can be on his team, but he will be limiting the number that

will be living with him and hearing his teaching on a daily basis. The group he picks will have the responsibility of teaching others all that he has said. It will be the most important team ever put together."

Priscilla interrupted, "It's too bad he has to limit the number at all. It seems like it should be 'the more the merrier.'"

"That's a good point, Priscilla. I guess it's just like it is in a family. If parents have lots of children, it's difficult to give time and attention to each one.

"Jesus wants to make sure the twelve he chooses will learn well. He knows that very soon these twelve will have to be good 'parents' to others, as will their 'children.'"

"But it still means that some of them won't make the team—not even as a right fielder—doesn't it?"

"That's right, Pete. At least not on this group of first-stringers. And that's why Jesus has those tears on his cheeks, and why you could hear a feather drop."

Then we heard Jesus say, "These are the twelve I have chosen:

Simon, ["Jesus later names him Peter," Jesna whispered.]
James, son of Zebedee,
John, brother of James, ["Jesus will nickname the Zebedee
    brothers, 'sons of thunder'," she whispered.
    "Whoa," Pete said, "that Zebedee must have a loud
    mouth."]
Andrew,
Philip,
Bartholomew,
Matthew, ["Hey, the tax-taker made it."]
Thomas,
James, son of Alphaeus,
Thaddaeus,
Simon the Canaanite, and
Judas Iscariot.

When the last name was called the ones who made the team
and the ones who did not exchanged hugs. Jesus invited everyone
to spend the night together on the mountain top and welcomed
those who were not chosen to visit often.

Then, as the small crowd began to set up camp, one of the
ones who was not chosen approached Jesus.

"Listen," Jesna said. She pointed to where Jesus stood with his
disappointed pupil.

"I'm Matthias."

"I know," Jesus said as he put a hand on his shoulder.

"I just want you to know that being with you these few weeks
has turned my life inside out. I want you to know that I'll still be
following you, though from a distance."

Jesus' smile became radiant as he said, "There will never be
much distance between you and me."

"Keep your eyes on that one," Jesna said to all four Pilgrims. "He's in for the same ride as you."

FAMILY DISCUSSION

1. Did you know that there were more than twelve who wanted to give up everything to follow Jesus?

2. How do you think it felt to be picked as a disciple? How do you think it felt not to be picked as part of the original group?

3. If you had lived back then would you have been willing to give up everything to follow Jesus? How about now?

SCENE FORTY-SIX
THE OCCASION OF THE SERMON ON THE MOUNT[76]

That evening Jesus sat with his friends by the light of a glowing campfire. After a while he began to teach about his favorite subject—his Father's kingdom. He told them that beginning now, they were all under a new Government, a holy Government.

Their job, he said, would be to tell the world that the gates to this "kingdom" are wide open to all. "Anyone who is willing to obey the rules of the King may live in his kingdom, and enjoy eating its fruits of love, righteousness, peace, and joy.

"Anyone," he said again, as he looked into the face of Matthias, and then into the faces of others who would not be traveling with him on a daily basis.

After a while the serious talk became more playful. It wasn't long after that until the campfire died down. Snores, loud and gargling, started going up. Mr. Pilgrim would have easily won a snoring contest—with Pete finishing a very respectable second.

The next morning we broke camp and headed back down the mountain. The crowd must have seen us from a distance and decided to meet us in the middle.

Jesus seemed excited that the crowd we had left the day before had not gone home. Instead, it had become a congregation marching our way.

Arriving at a quiet place, a natural amphitheater, Jesus sat down and waited for the crowd to gather.

When a group had amassed that would overflow most any high school football stadium, Jesus stood and began to teach them—continuing with his campfire lessons from the night before. This is what he said:

"You're blessed when you're at the end of your rope. With less of you there is more of God and his rule.

"You're blessed when you feel you've lost what is most dear to you. Only then can you be embraced by the One most dear to you.

"You're blessed when you're content with just who you are—no more, no less. That's the moment you find yourselves proud owners of everything that can't be bought.

"You're blessed when you've worked up a good appetite for God. He's food and drink in the best meal you'll ever eat.

"You're blessed when you care. At the moment of being 'care-full,' you find yourselves cared for.

"You're blessed when you get your inside world—your mind and heart—put right. Then you can see God in the out-side world.

"You're blessed when you can show people how to cooperate instead of compete or fight. That's when you discover who you really are, and your place in God's family.

"You're blessed when your commitment to God provokes persecution. The persecution drives you deeper into God's kingdom."[77]

Jesus paused to give his words a chance to settle into the ears of his listeners.

During the pause Mr. Pilgrim whispered to Jesna: "I don't get it. He seems to be saying that most of what we call a 'curse' is a blessing? It sounds like a fantasy world to me. I mean, that's just not the way business is done in the real world!"

Mrs. Pilgrim gave her husband's words a wide-eyed nod of agreement.

"Oh, you're right, Mr. Pilgrim," Jesna said. "The rules are as different as night and day in the two worlds—'His kingdom' and what you called the 'real world.' There is one thing, though, he might say you have backwards. It's the kingdom that is 'real.' It's all that really matters and what lasts forever. It's this world—yours and theirs—" (she said while giving a sweeping point at the crowd), "that's a passing fantasy. We'll all want to listen very carefully. He's going to tell us exactly how business is done in the 'real world,' and how to get on board."

FAMILY DISCUSSION

1. What do you think God's kingdom looks like?

2. What do you suppose Mr. Pilgrim was feeling when Jesus was teaching about who is really "blessed"?

3. As kingdom dwellers, how should we act differently than people who live in the "world"?

SCENE FORTY-SEVEN

SALT AND LIGHT[78]

Jesus continued his sermon from the mountainside. He was sitting on a large boulder flecked with chips of mica that sparkled in the morning sun. He was speaking in such a relaxed manner it was as if he were having a parlor conversation with a few close friends. But the strength of his voice told the truth. He was preaching to a multitude of special friends in one of his Father's large, outdoor living rooms.

The crowd was still and quiet. Thousands of pairs of dark brown eyes had become glued to his face in reverent stares. It seemed everyone knew that breaking a twig or crunching a leaf could cause people to miss a crucial word of Jesus' special invitation to leave their miserable worlds and enter into "The Kingdom" of his Father.

From the looks of the crowd I don't think many of them were being flooded with invitations, of any kind. They sure didn't want to miss this one.

Jesus continued:

"You are the salt of the earth; but if you have lost your flavor, how can it be restored? It is no longer good for anything except to be thrown out and trampled on by people.

"You are the light of the world. A city set on a hill cannot be hid. Let your light so shine before men, that they may see your good works and give glory to your Father who is in heaven."[79]

"I don't get it," Pete said in a sing-song voice. No one looked surprised.

"What don't you get, Pete?"

"Well, what's so great about being salt? I mean, I remember one time when I was visiting my grandparents who live on a farm, and one day, when no one was around, I walked out into the pasture and put a big lick on one of those big, square-looking salt licks—just like I had seen the cows do." (Mrs. Pilgrim gasped). "And it tasted real yucky. I mean it took me half a day to spit that taste out of my mouth. I don't know why Jesus would want people to be like that, making everybody gag?"

"What did it taste like?" Priscilla asked.

"Never mind that, young man. You just make sure you don't ever do something like that again."

"I know. I know. I could've gotten cowpox or something. But Jesus is saying that we are supposed to be like a salt lick. And maybe even the Pharisees are supposed to come by and lick us on the head. I'm just trying to understand it. It's sorta weird."

"May I interrupt?" Jesna asked.

"Please do," said Mrs. Pilgrim.

"Pete, have you ever eaten popcorn that didn't have any salt on it?"

"Yes, I have. Mom tries to slip stuff like that past us all the time. It's awful! I'd just as soon eat the box my sneakers came in! I'd rather kiss Priscilla than eat any more of that stuff!"

"Do you like popcorn with salt on it, Pete?"

"Oh, I love it. It tastes great—even better with butter and a good movie, though."

"So it took the salt to bring out the flavor that was already in the popcorn, but hidden. Right?"

"Yeah, I guess so."

"Well, Jesus is saying that people in his 'kingdom' are like salt. If they're absent, the world is like unsalted popcorn. If they are present, they cause all the God-flavors hidden in those around them, to come out. People in the world, lightly salted by kingdom kids, begin to 'taste' like love, peace, and joy. And pretty soon they want to live in the 'kingdom' too."

"So, Jesna, if you start living in the 'kingdom,' the best comes out of you and you begin to bring out the best in those around you?"

"That's right, Priscilla," Jesna answered. "You begin to bring out their best God-flavors. Their family and friends won't be able to eat enough of the changes, and everyone will see the value of becoming salt."

"It's the same with 'light' and 'darkness,'" Jesna continued. "Just as the first rays of dawn paint the world that had been so dull and grey only moments before with all the colors of an artist's palette, kingdom dwellers shine their light into the dark world and bring out all the hidden God-colors."

"Wow!" Pete said. "Salted popcorn and a movie. Where do I sign up?"

FAMILY DISCUSSION

1. How does it feel if someone is "salt" or "light" to *you*?

2. Have you ever been "salt" or "light" to someone else?

3. How did it make you feel?

SCENE FORTY-EIGHT
IT'S THE LAW[80]

Jesus stood up from his rock stage and began to stroll through the crowd, as he continued to teach. The wind was mild but constant. Often it would push a strand of brown hair across his face. But his eyes were undistracted.

Sometimes Jesus would stop, right next to a person in the audience, and place his hand on his shoulder. Sometimes he would speak while looking directly into the eyes of one individual, as he addressed everyone. But the crowd remained transfixed. Only Jesus and the wind made any noise. That is, until he said:

"Think not that I have come to abolish the law and the prophets; I have come not to abolish them but to fulfill them.

"...Whoever trivializes even the least of these (written) commandments and teaches others to do the same, shall be called least in the kingdom of heaven; but those who do them and show the way to others shall be called great in the kingdom of heaven.

"For I tell you, unless your righteousness exceeds that of the Scribes and the Pharisees, you will never enter the kingdom of heaven."[81]

When Jesus was saying the last of those words the crowd made its first noise. It let out a collective gasp. It certainly didn't escape Pete's attention.

"Wow! Did you feel that? Everybody sucked in so hard it almost turned my baseball cap around!"

"Yeah, Jesna," Priscilla echoed. "Why is everyone looking so shocked right now?"

"Well, they're all very excited to hear about 'the kingdom,' and I imagine most are seriously considering doing whatever Jesus says is necessary to start living in it.

"But he has just said something really shocking, that their 'righteousness' would have to be better than that of the Pharisees to get in. They probably can't imagine how anyone could be more righteous than the Pharisees."

"Yeah," Pete echoed, "they're professionals. I can almost hear one of those black-robed guys saying, 'Do not try this (to be like me) at home. I am a professional.'"

"But," Jesna continued, "do you know what it means to be righteous?"

All four Pilgrims shook their heads "No." I shook my head, too, but no one noticed.

"To be righteous simply means to 'live right,' to live out of a heart that has been set right.

"While the Pharisees do an incredible job of keeping all the law that is written in Scripture, and even some extra stuff that they made up themselves, they often do so with hearts that are harder than the stone the Ten Commandments were written on. Way too hard for God to write on."

Pete interrupted, "Sort of like if I were to go to bed on time every night, but stay up until after midnight listening to the radio under the covers, while grumbling to myself about all the stupid rules we have about bedtime. Not that I've actually done that."

"Exactly, Pete. Exactly," Jesna said.

"You see, God has given his children the law at least four times—each time on a softer tablet. He wrote the Ten

Commandments in stone, then the Torah on parchment, then he put it in the hearts and mouths of his prophets (as a reminder for those who missed the stone and paper versions), and finally, he sent it in the form of his own Son—in the flesh.

"Our ability to 'live right' exceeds that of the 'righteousness-professionals' when we allow God to write his Law a fifth time—on our hearts."

"And do you know what he always writes?"

Four Pilgrims again nodded a collective "No."

He writes, "Love me with all your heart, and love your neighbor as yourself."

"To allow this law to be written in flesh, on our hearts, changes nothing of what He has already written in stone and paper. And yet, it changes everything."

"So," Priscilla said, "let me see if I've got this. If our family rules were written on Pete's heart, instead of just on the refrigerator, he would go to bed every night at 8:30 without being asked because the heart-rule says he loves Mom and Dad, and knows that the rules are because they love him, too."

"That's right, Priscilla." Jesna said.

"Man," Pete exclaimed, "maybe it's easier to be a Pharisee!"

"You said it, little 'black-robed guy.'"

FAMILY DISCUSSION

1. Why do you think Jesus' words about right living were so hard for the Pharisees to hear?

2. How would it feel different for Pete to have the family rules written on his heart, instead of attached to the refrigerator?

3. How would he act differently, if he were following heart rules?

SCENE FORTY-NINE
SO MAD YOU COULD KILL[82]

Fluffy, white clouds, unusual for this season, drifted across a blue sky like slow-moving spaceships. This caused billowy shadows to pass over the crowd, which still sat motionless before Jesus.

From the spaceship clouds, the people probably looked like a huge, multicolored glove, with long, spindly fingers, that some giant had abandoned. It was a "glove" that was certainly trying to catch every word that Jesus tossed out. But then, he threw them a curve:

"You're familiar with the command to the ancients, 'Do not murder.' I'm telling you that anyone who is so much as angry with a brother or sister is guilty of murder."

Pete gasped.

"Carelessly call a brother 'idiot!' And you just might find yourself hauled into court."

Priscilla gasped.

"Thoughtlessly yell 'stupid!' at a sister and you are on the brink of hellfire."

"I think I'm going to be sick," Pete said.

"The simple moral fact is that words kill.
"This is how I want you to conduct yourself in these matters. If you enter your place of worship and, about to make an

offering, you suddenly remember a grudge a friend has against you, abandon your offering, leave immediately, go to this friend and make things right. Then and only then, come back and work things out with God."[83]

"Jesna!" Mr. Pilgrim said as beads of perspiration were forming on his forehead. "How can anyone live life without ever losing their temper and calling someone a name?"

"My thought exactly!" Pete said. "Nobody can keep from calling his sister 'stupid.' I don't think I've made it for a whole day without saying that. I mean, sometimes she IS 'stupid.'"

"Uh-oh, my little 'idjut' brother, you're going to fry for that one."

"Yeah? Well you just called me an 'idjut.' You're in even worse trouble than I am!"

"You see what I mean, Jesna," Mr. Pilgrim said, his forehead a little dryer now. "It seems like Jesus has set the high jump bar way too high, don't you think?"

"No, I don't," Jesna said. "I do see what you are saying, and why you are saying it." (She gave Pete and Priscilla a quick glance.) "But you have to understand what Jesus is doing here. He's still making the case that in the 'kingdom' there is a whole new way of being righteous, uh, 'living right.'

"Everyone in the crowd knows what has been written in stone, 'Thou shall not kill.' But a person can keep that commandment while having a heart that has been turned to stone by his or her anger for someone. And he or she can keep the commandment not to kill while hating that person and murdering his reputation, with gossip—every day.

"But hatred and reputation murder can't happen if you have the two supreme commandments written in flesh—on your heart. Because if you are truly head over heels in love with God, your real Daddy, and you truly love your neighbor (all your neighbors) as yourself, you will keep both the easy commandment—don't murder—and the harder ones—don't hate or insult.

"But Jesus isn't saying this to try to make people feel guilty. He's trying to motivate them to move away from the world of anger and competition and into his Father's kingdom of selfless love. Nothing, not even giving a present to God in church, is more important than keeping the commandments to love.

"And you're right, Mr. Pilgrim. He has set the high jump bar real, real high. No one can possibly make it over the top unless he crawls up on God's back and jumps from his shoulders."

Pete must have done just that. Because when Jesna finished talking, he was giving his sister a hug.

FAMILY DISCUSSION

1. What do you think Jesus meant by saying, "words kill"?

2. Have you ever been stabbed by someone's words? How did it leave you feeling?

3. God helped Pete hug his sister. Can you describe in words what you think Pete's heart felt like when he did that?

SCENE FIFTY
WATCH OUT, DANGER AHEAD[84]

Pete let Priscilla loose from the bear hug he had thrown around her. She looked as surprised as a cat that has just been licked by a bulldog.

"Humm," Pete mused. "That was more fun than calling you a name."

Priscilla took two steps backward and her surprised eyes widened, pulling her head an extra step back.

"Listen," Mr. Pilgrim whispered, "Jesus is teaching about something else."

"Let's not pretend this is easier than it really is. If you want to live a morally pure life, here's what you have to do: You have to blind your right eye the moment you catch it in a lustful leer. You have to choose to live one-eyed or else be dumped on a moral trash pile. And you have to chop off your right hand the moment you notice it raised threateningly. Better a bloody stump than your entire being discarded for good in the dump."[85]

"Whoa, Dad! This is beginning to sound like some of those horror movies you won't let us watch. You know, like, 'Nightmare on Galilee Street,' or something."

"Hush, Son," Mr. Pilgrim said, "Jesus might hear you talking sacrin-religious like that."

"That's sacrilegious, Dear." Mrs. Pilgrim corrected.

"Sacrin, scri-, either way it's not the real thing."

Pete was looking a little scared. He was squeezing his upper arms with his palms. "You d-d-don't think J-J-Jesus will cut off my arms d-d-do you?"

Jesna couldn't stop a laugh from jumping right out of her throat. Some words somersaulted out just behind it. "Pete, you're incredible. But I do wonder if you have any idea what kind of love Jesus is made of."

She continued as Pete gave his upper arms reassuring pats. "Let me ask you a question. If you saw your family driving down a mountain road in their car, all laughing and smiling, radio playing, but not realizing that around the next curve the bridge had been washed out, and there were no warning signs; what would you do?"

"Am I in a helicopter?"

"Humm?"

"I mean, how could I not be in the car and still see them. I think I would need to be in a helicopter."

"OK, Pete. You're in a helicopter. Now, what would you do?"

"Well I would make that helicopter dive down right beside them, or in front of them," (he demonstrated with his hand as he talked) "and I'd holler, 'STOP! YOU CAN'T GO THIS WAY! YOU'RE GOING TO DIE!'"

"What if they didn't see you?"

"I'd sit on the helicopter horn and blow it until they looked at me. Then, when I had their attention, I'd yell, 'DANGER!' 'STOP!' That's what I'd do—Whatever it would take to get their attention and stop them."

"What if they couldn't hear you yelling because of all the helicopter noise?"

"I'd show them a picture of a wrecked car, and point at it, and then at them."

"Well, Pete, it sounds like you'd do just what Jesus is doing."

"Huh?"

"He sees that his family—all these people—are headed for a cliff. And they don't know it, either. To make matters worse, the religious leaders of the day have almost everybody convinced that the road they are on leads to heaven. 'Just don't break any of the big rules, try to be almost as righteous as us, and you'll probably be OK.' But actually, that way to heaven has a bridge missing."

"The bridge is Jesus, right?"

"That's right, Pete. The bridge is Jesus, who laid down his life for them all. But before he did, Jesus tried to show the people who were following those religious leaders that they were heading for a "dead end." Jesus showed them a few pictures of their wrecked lives to shock them and get their attention. And then he told the truth. It IS better to travel *his* road, even with a headlight missing, than to go the wrong way where there is no bridge..."

"'Cause you might crash and burn?"

"That's right, Pete. And while cars and headlights don't matter so much, people and their souls do."

FAMILY DISCUSSION

1. Why do you think Jesus was trying to shock the people?

2. What do you suppose it would feel like to be in a car headed for a cliff?

3. How would you act toward someone if he saved you from falling off a cliff?

SCENE FIFTY-ONE
DON'T SWEAR[86]

Jesus continued to stroll through his audience. As he walked, his hands were often busy—patting the back of an adult or brushing the face of a child. His words, however, were becoming increasingly less gentle.

"You have heard it said, 'you should not swear falsely, but should perform to the Lord what you have sworn.' But I tell you now, do not swear at all, either by heaven, for it is the throne of God, or by the earth, for it is his footstool, or by Jerusalem, for it's the city of the great king. And do not swear by your head, for you can't make one hair on it white or black. Let what you say be simply 'yes' or 'no'; anything more than this comes from the devil—the enemy of life in the kingdom."[87]

"Jesna?"

"Yes, Priscilla."

"What does it mean to swear? I always thought swearing meant saying a bad word. But Jesus seems to be talking about something different."

"Yes, he is. Swearing in Bible times didn't mean cursing, it meant taking an oath. An oath is calling on God to witness that what you are saying is true. It's very serious and there are a lot of formulas for how to do them right." Priscilla's eyes always sparkled when she heard words like "formulas."

"Usually," Jesna went on, "when someone makes an oath he or she is inviting God to kill him or her, or the one with whom the oath is made, if that person isn't telling the truth."

"Well, Jesna, why is Jesus preaching against them? I mean, if everybody is doing it, and it's a way to make sure you mean what you are promising?"

"I think, Priscilla, Jesus would say that there are at least two things that are really wrong with making oaths like that. First, it assumes that you can tell God what to do."

"And who to kill," Pete interrupted.

"And that," Jesna continued, "means you are acting like you are equal to God. That's what got Adam and Eve kicked out of the garden of Eden—trying to be God. Secondly, it assumes you don't usually tell the truth—and that if you are it's a really big deal. The current religious system…"

"The one the Pharisees are first-string players in?"

"That's right, Pete. In that system—the only one these people know anything about—it's OK to take an oath. You're just supposed to keep the promises you are swearing to keep. But that's also like saying, 'It's OK that everyone has a hard and deceitful heart.'

"Jesus is saying that if you are a citizen of the kingdom, your heart is filled with love, and you wouldn't even think about telling a lie to get the best of someone. If you love everybody as yourself, there is no thought of getting ahead of your neighbor. What's good for them is good for you, and vice versa.

"In one system it's assumed that hearts are hard and impure and that it would take the fear of death to get you to actually tell the truth. In the other system, the 'kingdom,' it's assumed that hearts are soft and pure and that a falsehood would be as out of place in your mouth as…"

"A fish on a bicycle?" Pete interrupted.

"Yes, Pete, 'a fish on a bicycle.'"

"So," he continued. "In the kingdom 'yes' means 'yes' and 'no' means 'no,' and there's no need to ask God to punch you in the face, if you were lying, because you won't be."

"You got it."

FAMILY DISCUSSION

1. How would you describe to a friend how Jesus' system of telling the truth is better than the old one of swearing oaths?

2. Can we ever tell God what to do? What are we really saying when we try?

SCENE FIFTY-TWO
I'LL GET EVEN[88]

Jesus completed his circle through the crowd and arrived back at the sparkling boulder where he had begun his sermon.

"You know," Jesna said, "we are all getting to witness the greatest sermon ever preached."

Mr. and Mrs. Pilgrim nodded in agreement.

"Well, I sure like that it's outdoors," Pete said. "If you get bored you can always pick up a rock or an ant or something." But Pete hadn't picked up anything (not even his foot) since Jesus spoke the first words of the sermon.

"I've never seen him so still and quiet before—even when he's asleep," his father said.

Jesus had suddenly become quiet. He surveyed the crowd with a gaze. It was as if he weren't sure we were ready to hear what came next. Then, he began again:

"Here's another old saying that deserves a second look: 'Eye for eye, tooth for tooth.' Is that going to get us anywhere? Here's what I propose: 'Don't hit back at all.' If someone strikes you, stand there and take it. If someone drags you into court and sues for the shirt off your back, giftwrap your best coat and make a present of it. And if someone takes unfair advantage of you, use the occasion to practice the servant life. No more tit-for-tat stuff. Live generously.

"You're familiar with the old written law, 'Love your friend,' and its unwritten companion, 'Hate your enemy.' I'm challenging that. I'm telling you to love your enemies. Let them bring out the best in you, not the worst. When someone gives you a hard time, respond with the energies of prayer, for then you are working out of your true selves, your God-created selves. This is what God does."[89]

Pete spoke for the crowd. "Jesna, I like Jesus and everything, but he's got to be kidding here. There is a punch line coming, right? I mean, I want to know where the line is that if a bully crosses it I can punch him out."

"There's no punch line coming, Pete. And no lines for punching, either."

"But, if I acted like he wants me to... uh... I'd be a sissy. No offense, Prissy, but I'd be a girl."

"This isn't a boy-girl thing, little brother. I don't like what I'm hearing either.

"Just last week at school, a girl who makes fun of me for always getting A's tore the plastic cover off my term paper, just before I was supposed to turn it in."

"What did you do to her?"

"Well, I ripped the first page off her paper (she didn't have a nice plastic cover). And even the teacher said that I had the right to do that."

"Gimme five, Prissy, I didn't know you had it in you."

"You're right, Priscilla," Jesna said, ignoring Pete and the pop of two hands slapping. "We have every right to hurt back, when we are hurt."

"Well, OK then," Priscilla said, as her lips formed a smug smile. "Then there *is* a punch line, here. When is Jesus going to tell us about that?"

"If you insist on one, here it is: The kingdom is not about being within your rights; it's about becoming righteous. You don't become righteous by grabbing your rights. You become righteous by giving them away."

This caused Pete and Priscilla's smiles to turn upside down.

"But no one can do that," Priscilla said, as she punched at her wrist computer. "It's just not part of human nature."

"That's right, Priscilla. No one can do it—at least not for very long—on their own. It can only be done by giving up and inviting Jesus to come and live in your heart to do it through you. And then asking him a thousand times to do it."

"I knew there was a punch line!" Pete said, as his lips inverted again.

"In a word," [Jesus said, now returning Pete's smile] "what I'm saying is, *Grow up*. You're kingdom subjects. Now live like it. Live out your God-created identity. Live generously and graciously toward others, the way God lives toward you."[90]

Priscilla was still staring at her computer and shaking her head. "Everything he's saying goes against human nature. A person would have to become a whole new person to be able to do as he says."

"Right!" Jesna said. "A whole new Jesus-in-you-and-acting-through-you person. But it's a small price to pay for becoming princes and princesses in Jesus' kingdom."

FAMILY DISCUSSION

1. Tell what it was like when you were kind to someone who was expecting you to be mean.

2. What do you suppose Jesus meant when he said "Grow up"?

3. What does it feel like to let Jesus live *his* life through *you*?

SCENE FIFTY-THREE
DO GOOD, BUT DON'T BRAG[91]

Jesus unlocked his eyes from Pete's and continued his message:

"Be especially careful when you are trying to be good so that you don't make a performance out of it. It might be good theater, but the God who made you won't be applauding.

"...When you do something for someone else, don't call attention to yourself.... Just do it—quietly and unobtrusively. That is the way your God, who conceived you in love, working behind the scenes, helps you out."[92]

"Ya' know," Pete whispered to Jesna, "I've got a friend who always makes a big deal out of it when he does something good."

"Is that right, Pete?"

"Oh, yeah. Like when we are playing basketball and he makes a shot, he always struts around like a rooster on hot coals. And he *always* looks all around to see if anybody was watching. Shoot! Lots of times the person he was supposed to be guarding scores a basket while he's still strutting. I'm sure glad Jesus is getting on his case! I think I'll tell him Jesus was preaching against him when we get back home."

"So you don't like to be on the same team with him?" Jesna asked.

"What 'team'? He wouldn't know a team if it jumped him. He's just out there for himself—to impress folks."

"But," Pete continued, "I don't see why it matters to Jesus if this guy is a 'glory hound.'"

"Maybe it's because they don't allow 'hot dogs' in the kingdom," Jesna answered.

"What! No hot dogs?" (My ears perked up; this conversation was getting interesting.)

"Relax, little brother; it's a metaphor. Do you know what a metaphor is?"

"Yeah, a meadow is for grazing cows. But I'm wanting to know if I can eat hot dogs at Jesus' place. Because if I can't..."

"Ahhh-h-h-hum." Jesna said, clearing her throat. "In the Kingdom you can eat all the hot dogs your parents will allow. You just can't *be* one.

"'Hot dogs,' like your friend, are more focused on themselves than on others. And one of the first two rules of the kingdom is to love your neighbor as much as you love yourself. That's why kingdom-living basketball players are just as likely to pass the ball as to shoot it and much more likely to pat their teammates on the back than to try to pat their own."

"So," Pete said, "Jesus won't be letting my friend the 'hot dog' come and mess up any of the basketball games in his kingdom, then. He'll lock the gym door right in his face, huh?"

"Not exactly, Pete. It's more likely Jesus will leave the gym door wide open. He would probably invite your friend to come over and sit on his lap for a long, long time, until he felt loved and cared for, deep down inside, and wasn't so starving for attention. Then, when he's ready to be a team member, Jesus would put him in the game and be his loudest cheerleader. You see, when you move into the kingdom you always get back whatever you were willing to give up."

"I think I get it, Jesna," Pete said, as a 'watch-out' smile shot across his face. "But I still don't *relish* being on a former 'hot dog's' team. Get it, Priscilla?" he said as he gave her a nudge in the ribs. "Now *that's* a pun-ny metaphor."

Even Jesna groaned.

FAMILY DISCUSSION

1. In what ways would you like to receive more attention in your family?

2. In what ways can you be more of an attention giver?

3. What does it mean to pray, "To God be the glory"?

SCENE FIFTY-FOUR
THE LORD'S PRAYER[93]

Jesus stopped talking. He allowed the pause after his last paragraph to grow into an uncomfortably long silence. A few nervous ripples of movement began to spread across the sea of listeners. Then Jesus walked behind the big rock he had been standing in front of and took one giant step to the top of it.

"I want to talk to you about something very special." His words immediately stilled the waves.

"Did you know that you can talk to God, your heavenly Father, anytime? Did you know that he listens to you—whenever you talk with him—with the love of a 'Daddy' for his small child? Did you know that he knows you by name, by the sound of your voice, by the hairs on your head, and that he longs to talk to you? So talk with him! He wants you to. Ask him any question and expect an answer. But do it the right way.

"If you were going to have a conversation with your husband or wife, you wouldn't go out to the public square and shout, 'I'M GOING TO TALK TO MY WIFE NOW!' Or if you wanted to ask your parents for advice you wouldn't put on your finest clothes and spend half an hour heaping empty praises on them, like, 'OH, GRACIOUS PARENTS WHO ARE MORE BRIGHT AND SHINY THAN THE SUN AND FROM WHOSE LOINS I AM PRIVILEGED TO HAVE SPRUNG...'

"No! You would want to talk with them in private and you would want to share with them from a sincere and loving heart. It's the same when you talk with your heavenly Father. Don't do as the hypocrites who pretend to pray but are only sincere about their desire to be seen and heard by others.

"Real prayer doesn't come from grinding our teeth, but from falling in love."

Then Jesus stepped back down from the rock, went back around to the front of it, and sat down. When the crowd began to shift and move to be able to see him, he said, "Please, sit with me and close your eyes." The mountain groaned at the impact of several thousand people, sitting down at once.

After a long silence, and with his own eyes gently closed, this is what we heard Jesus say:

> "Our Father in heaven,
> holy and sacred is your name.
> May your kingdom come,
> may your will be done,
> on earth as it is in heaven.
> Give us this day the food we need;
> and forgive us our sins against you
> as we forgive others;
> keep us safe from ourselves
> and from the Devil.[94]
>
> "You are in charge!
> You can do anything you want!
> You're ablaze in beauty![95]
> Amen, Father."

When Jesus had finished his conversation with his Father he was silent for a long time. No one interrupted. No one asked what he heard back. But whatever it was, it made him smile.

FAMILY DISCUSSION

1. Please take the time to pray slowly the Lord's Prayer as a family.

2. Now pray it even more slowly to yourself, saying only a few words as you slowly breathe in and out.

3. Tell the others about any new thoughts, feelings, or mental pictures you had as you slowly prayed the Lord's Prayer.

SCENE FIFTY-FIVE
TREASURES, HEARTS, AND SERVING TWO MASTERS[96]

After a while Jesus opened his eyes and continued his sermon. There was nothing on his face to indicate that he had just finished talking with the Maker of mountains. The crowd remained seated.

"Don't hoard treasure down here where it gets eaten by moths and corroded by rust or—worse!—stolen by burglars. Stockpile treasure in heaven, where it's safe from moth and rust and burglars. It's obvious, isn't it? The place where your treasure is, is the place you will most want to be, and end up being.

"Your eyes are windows into your body. If you open your eyes wide in wonder and belief, your body fills up with light. If you live squinty-eyed in greed and distrust, your body is a dank cellar.

"You can't worship two gods at once. Loving one god, you'll end up hating the other. Adoration of one feeds contempt for the other. You can't worship God and Money both."[97]

"Wait a minute! Wait a minute, Jesna," Mr. Pilgrim exclaimed. "I'm still trying to digest what he said about how I should run my business. He's not going to tell me that there's something wrong with making money, is he?"

"Oh, certainly not, Mr. Pilgrim. Jesus doesn't have any problem with people working and making money. He himself worked as a carpenter for almost twenty years. And he didn't usually work for free.

"He is saying that you must be careful not to value money too highly—not worship it—or you will end up living in its fast-fading kingdom and not God's."

"But Jesna, how can you avoid valuing something that is valuable?"

"Let me try to explain with a story—actually a scene from a wonderful book, called *Lilith*.[98] At one point in the book Mr. Vane, he's the main character, has journeyed through a mirror into a whole new world, and has become a slave to a group of giants. During the days, while the giants are away, he meets and makes friends with a tribe of Lilliputian-sized people called the 'little ones.' He discovers that the 'little ones' are as joyful and carefree as the giants are sad and self-centered.

"One day he is talking to one of the 'little ones' about where giants come from. He is told by 'Tolma,' his little friend, that the giants were once 'little ones' themselves. In fact, she says, giants are 'little ones' who have lost themselves and now think of nothing but eating and growing big. When they cannot grow any bigger, they try to grow fatter. Giants in that land are those who have become obsessed with eating and themselves.

"Mr. Vane comments, 'So [it is] in my world, only they do not say *fat* there, they say *rich*.'

"You see, Mr. Pilgrim, the 'little ones' eat food too, and enjoy it quite a lot. But the 'giants' have made eating their reason to live. They view their bigness as a great accomplishment. And they see every other mouth as a threat to their superiority.

"The 'giants' look at the world through 'squinty-eyes,' in greed and distrust. If they would just open them wider they would be able to see that they have made a god out of what was meant to be a gift from God."

"And," Pete interrupted, while blowing on the end of his fore-finger as if he had just fired a six-shooter, "There's room in this universe for only one God, partner."

"That's right, Pete. And if we see *him* as the real treasure, *our* real treasure, we will end up being with him, instead of with his competitors—because we will have spent time with what we value most."

"Well, Jesna," Mr. Pilgrim said, "you and Jesus have opened *my* eyes a bit wider."

FAMILY DISCUSSION

1. What does it mean to store up treasures in heaven?

2. How can you go about putting "money" into that account?

SCENE FIFTY-SIX
DON'T PANIC[99]

The wind had shifted, bringing with it half a sky full of puffy white clouds. The late afternoon sun had set fire to the bottoms of several of the clouds. Their tops were still cool gray. A potpourri of smells also caught a ride with the wind. The best smell was the sweet scent of the freshly pruned grapevines, blown up from the hill side below. To my dog nose, the aroma of spice and herbs from a distant caravan was a close second, although I was not sure it could be enjoyed by people-noses. It helped me to ignore the unwanted smell being blown in from the hundreds of humans.

Jesus was intent on bringing change into an invisible world. He continued to speak without acknowledging the rapid changes in the world all around us:

> "If you decide for God, living a life of God-worship, it follows that you don't fuss about what's on the table at mealtimes or whether the clothes in your closet are in fashion. There is far more to your life than the food you put in your stomach, more to your outer appearance than the clothes you hang on your body. Look at the birds, free and unfettered, not tied down to a job description, careless in the care of God. And you count far more to him than birds.
>
> "...If God gives such attention to the appearance of wild-flowers—most of which are never even seen—don't you think he'll attend to you, take pride in you, do his best for you? What I'm trying to do here is to get you to relax, to not be so preoccupied with *getting*, so you can respond to God's *giving*....

Don't worry about missing out. You'll find all your everyday human concerns will be met.

"The Father wants to give you the very kingdom itself."[100]

"Did you hear what he said, Mom? He wants everybody to chill. Man, I wish your sister, Aunt Bessy, could hear that. She's the most unrelaxed person I ever saw!"

"Pete, that's not a very nice thing to say about your aunt. She's not *that* anxious."

"Oh, yeah, she is! When we're over at her house she never sits down. She's always busy—cleaning or cooking or offering us stuff. And she moves real fast and talks real fast, too. I bet she could get on a hound dog's nerves."

"That'll be enough about your Aunt Bessy, Son. She does the best she can to relax. It's just not easy for her."

"If I may interrupt?" Jesna asked. "Jesus isn't talking about being anxious like that. I mean, some people were just born with engines that idle a little faster than most others. He's talking about not being able to relax because you've made a really big mistake; you've given away something very special and very valuable to someone you don't trust."

"What do you mean?"

"Well, Pete, what is the most valuable thing you own?"

"That's easy, my limited edition rookie baseball card of Ken Griffey, Jr. It's already worth more than $100.00. Right, Dad?"

"That's right, Pete, at least that much."

"Where is it now, Pete?"

"I gave it to my parents for safekeeping." Then he leaned over and whispered to Jesna, "Don't tell Priscilla this, but it's pressed between the pages of the 'X' volume of our encyclopedia. It's between page four and five because that's how old I was when I got it. Nobody will ever look in the 'X' encyclopedia."

"What if you took the card out?"

"Out of the encyclopedia or out of the house?" Pete said with a troubled look on his face, and then he clamped his hand over his mouth and said, "Oops!"

"Both. Out of the book, out of the house, and to school?"

"I-I wouldn't do that. Somebody might tear it or something. Especially Harley Davidson. That's his real name. He's named after a motorcycle. Harley would definitely tear it up!"

"What if you *gave* the card to Harley?"

"I wouldn't! I wouldn't even give any of *Priscilla's* stuff to him!"

"But if you did, Pete, how would you feel?"

"I'd be REAL worried all the time until I got it back. It wouldn't be safe with him. A pit bull in a motorcycle helmet wouldn't be safe with him!"

"Well, that's what Jesus has been preaching about."

"He's been preaching about Harley?"

"No. He's been preaching about how hard it is to relax when someone or something you don't trust owns your valuable possessions."

"Huh?" several voices said at once.

"If you trust money, fashion, or things you can buy to make you feel valuable, you'll be as anxious as Pete would be if Harley had his baseball card, because if you lose those things, you lose your feeling of worth."

"So, Jesna, Jesus is telling everyone to get their baseball cards back and give them to their parents for safekeeping?"

"Yes! He is saying that the only way to relax is to know that your Father, your heavenly Father, owns you, and you are very valuable to him."

"I bet he keeps it in the 'S' volume, for 'soul' huh? I bet he puts it on the page number that's our age when we give it to him. Do you think so, Jesna?"

"Wherever he puts them Pete, you don't have to worry about their getting lost."

"Maybe I'll ask Jesus to hang on to my baseball card, too. No offense, Dad."

"None taken. I've got a few things I might want him to hold on to for me."

FAMILY DISCUSSION

1. How does it make you feel to know that Jesus cares more about you than all the birds and flowers he created?

2. Have you ever felt deeply relaxed in God?

3. Tell how that felt. Then tell what caused the relaxed feeling to leave.

SCENE FIFTY-SEVEN
SPECKS AND LOGS[101]

No one asked Mr. Pilgrim what he meant when he said there were a few things he might want to give to Jesus for safekeeping. But the inquisitive looks on their faces showed they would love to know. From the satisfied smile on Jesna's face it appeared she already did know and was very pleased.

Jesus continued:

"Don't pick on people, jump on their failures, criticize their faults—unless, of course, you want the same treatment. Don't condemn those who are down; that hardness can boomerang. Be easy on people; you'll find life a lot easier. Give away your life; you'll find life given back, but not merely given back—given back with bonus and blessing. Giving, not getting, is the way. Generosity begets generosity."[102]

"Why do you become obsessed with the speck in someone else's eye but do not notice the log in your own eye? How can you say to the one with the speck, 'Friend, let me take that out for you,' when you do not see the log that is in your own eye?"[103]

"Now that's pretty funny," Pete said. "Can you imagine having a big old pine tree or something growing right outta your eyeball? I mean you'd be knocking stuff over every time you looked around. What would it be like if somebody with a tree-head tried to get a speck out of a normal person's eye? 'Uh, let me help you with that; SMACK!, Oh, sorry about the limb upside your head! I was just trying to help you.' That Jesus, he cracks me up sometimes."

"I don't think it's so funny, Pete," said Priscilla. "That's what you do to me all the time. You're always telling me what you think I'm doing wrong, not ever thinking that you might be a lumber-head."

"I didn't say I agreed with him, Speck, I mean Spock. I just said it was a funny way to talk. If you're doing something stupid, I'd think you would want to know."

Jesna was sucking in some air for a comment when Mrs. Pilgrim spoke.

"I think what Jesus is saying should make us all stop and think. We all criticize each other too much in this family. And whoever is doing the criticizing, myself included, is acting like a blockhead."

"What do you mean, Mom?" Pete asked.

"Well, when you criticize somebody, you are judging him. And, well, where does the judge sit in a courtroom?"

"Anywhere he wants. He is running the show."

"That's right, Pete. He can sit anywhere. And where he usually sits is on a platform, above the crowd, above everybody else, behind a big, high, wooden desk."

"So what's your point, Mom? You're beginning to scare me. You're sounding like Jesna. Oh, no offense, Jesna."

"None taken," said a still smiling Jesna. "I'm only the tour guide until you can do a self-guided tour. You were saying, Mrs. Pilgrim?"

"I was saying that the judge isn't on the same level with everybody else. He's above everyone else. When we judge, criticize, or condemn somebody, we're acting as if we are superior—better somehow.

"But that goes against everything we have been learning from Jesus. We are to love others as equals, not condemn them as judge and executioner. If we judge others, it's no wonder that they do the same to us, and climb up in the judge's chair the first chance they get!"

"But if we give out love, understanding, and hugs, that's what we'll get back instead of judgment."

"Mom."

"Yes, Pete."

"You're going to make a great tour guide."

FAMILY DISCUSSION

1. For the next few days try to stop yourself before any criticism of someone else, especially gossip. Then after apologizing for the unasked-for advice, ask Jesus to tell you about any "specks" you may have that need removing.

2. That might be a good time to confess any "logs" you know about that are sticking out of your eye. (But avoid any "speck" observations concerning anyone else while you are confessing.)

SCENE FIFTY-EIGHT
JUST ASK![104]

The gentle wind was still blowing in the same direction. The late-afternoon sun was making the color in Jesus' face a deep tan. He continued his sermon:

"Ask, and you will receive; seek, and you will find; knock, and it will be opened to you."

"Is this a riddle?" Pete asked.
"Shhh!" Both parents responded.

"For everyone who asks receives, and he who seeks finds, and to the one who knocks, it will be opened. Or which of you, if your child asks for bread, will give him a stone?"

"You know the bread and the stones look alike around here."
"Pete. Be quiet!" It sounded like Dad meant it.

"Or if your child asks for a fish, which of you would give him a snake? If you would give good gifts instead of cruel ones, how much more will your heavenly Father give you good things when you ask him!"[105]

"Pssst! Jesna."

"Yes, Priscilla."

"This is a little hard to talk about. But one time when I was a whole lot younger, real young, about Pete's age, I asked God for something, and, uh, I didn't get it. I didn't even get a rock or a snake."

"What did you ask for?"

"Well, it's kind of silly. And its sorta like something that Pete would ask for...." Pete was all ears. "I asked God for a chocolate Easter bunny, just a stupid little Easter bunny, but I didn't get it. It made me real mad."

"Wow, Priscilla. I never pictured you as a bunny-believer."

"I didn't ask the Easter Bunny, Pete; I asked God. But I still didn't get it. And Jesus just said you'd get what you ask for. But I didn't when *I* asked."

A tear was peeking over the ledge of Priscilla's left eye. I think it was the first one I had ever seen there. I think it was the first since she was a baby.

"It was about that time when I started to get interested in computers," Priscilla continued. "I figured if I couldn't count on God I'd have to start counting on stuff I *could* believe in, stuff you can count—facts and numbers."

Now Mr. and Mrs. Pilgrim had tears in their eyes.

Jesna reached over and touched Priscilla on the arm. "It's very hard to know why things work out the way they do sometimes. I'm sure I don't know.

"Maybe it's like it is with your earthly parents. They would prefer that you eat fruit and vegetables—because they love you and want you to grow strong—but sometimes they let you eat candy—because they know it makes you smile. But if you only ate candy, you'd die."

"Or turn into Pete," Priscilla interjected with a forced smile.

"I think it can be the same way with God. He wants us to have what will make us strong, even if we prefer to avoid what's good for us."

"Like asparagus?"

"Yes, Pete. Like asparagus. Or difficult things in life that we can learn from."

"But sometimes he can't resist doing something for us just to see the smile on our face."

"And that's when we get the chocolate?"

"I guess you could say that, Pete."

"So Priscilla, it's hard to predict what God will do. It's hard to know when he'll answer our prayer for 'chocolate' or when he'll send us a plate of asparagus. But whatever is set before us we should clean our plate and give thanks to our loving parent in heaven."

"I think I see what you're saying, Jesna, but he said if you asked for bread you would never get a rock."

"Bread's not chocolate, Priscilla. Chocolate is a treat that tastes great, but we don't really need it. If a child is asking for bread, that child is truly hungry. And while what Jesus is saying applies to eating real food, he's really still talking about his Father's kingdom. If we truly want to live there, and we ask to move there, then our prayer will surely be answered."

"Jesna," Priscilla said as she dabbed at the tear in her eye, "so sometimes you get chocolate and sometimes you don't, but you can have God's kingdom anytime?"

"That's right," Jesna said while slipping her arm around Priscilla's waist to give her a hug. "Sometimes Easter bunnies, *always* Easter mornings."

FAMILY DISCUSSION

1. What are the things that make it the most difficult for you to believe that God will answer your prayers for 'chocolate' or to live in his kingdom?

2. Have you ever had a disappointment like Priscilla's? Tell about it.

3. Ask those listening to your story to pray for you about how you might be comforted. Receive God's comfort through your family.

SCENE FIFTY-NINE
THE GOLDEN RULE[106]

"Now," Jesus said in a very loud voice, "I have something to tell all of you that is truly the most important thing I will say today." He paused. "If you want to know how to live in my Father's kingdom, if you want to know how to behave:

"Ask yourself what you want people to do for you, then grab the initiative and do it for *them*. Add up God's Law and Prophets and this is what you get."[107]

"All of Scripture is summarized in this rule. Chisel it on your hearts. Cast it in gold. And refer to it often. When you are not obeying this rule you are outside of the kingdom."

"Wow!" said Mr. Pilgrim. "Did you hear that, Dear? That's the 'golden rule,' that's the summary of his sermon. It's a summary of the whole Bible! Priscilla! Pete! Did you two hear that? Hey! Where are you?"

I looked around. Priscilla and Pete were both gone. There was nothing left where they had been standing but four foot prints on bent grass.

I began to sniff around. Salt water. Spices. Israelites. Canaanites. Cat trails. Oh! There they are. They had walked back to the car. In five or six giant dog leaps I was back at their sides, wagging my tail and listening.

"Priscilla," Pete said. His voice was low and serious, "I feel really bad about your not getting a chocolate Easter bunny when you were little. And, uh, I've been thinking. I got something I've been saving to take home. And, well, you can have it." Pete pulled a crumpled brown and white bag out of his side pocket.

"Oh Pete! Are you serious? *You* are going to give *me* an *M & M*? Your favorite candy?"

"No. Not one. You can have the whole half-bag that's left. They're *all* yours."

Then, just like that, another tear tried to push out of Priscilla's eye, the second one in just a few minutes. Priscilla reached out and took the gift from Pete as if it were a sack of diamonds. She knew that to Pete it was. Then, after staring at the black band on her wristwatch for a long time, she started to pick at it.

"Pete. Do you want to see how this wrist computer works?"

"DO I?" Pete exclaimed.

Mr. Pilgrim arrived just in time to see Priscilla holding Pete's treasure and Pete gently pressing the buttons to Priscilla's most prized possession.

"Oh my!" Mr Pilgrim exclaimed, "I guess you *did* hear him!"

FAMILY DISCUSSION

1. Why do you think Jesus said the "golden rule" summarizes the law and the prophets?

2. Pick out one person and tomorrow try to live out the "golden rule" with him or her.

3. The next day, pick two people.

SCENE SIXTY
THE TWO WAYS, ROCK OR SAND[108]

Mrs. Pilgrim joined her family back at the car. Jesna told them, "You might as well climb in. Jesus is just about to give the grand finale to the greatest sermon ever preached. Then, we're off again."

We all climbed in and listened to the last few paragraphs of Jesus' sermon from the mountainside. Being back in the car made it seem like we were watching a drive-in movie.

"Don't look for shortcuts to God. The market is flooded with sure-fire, easygoing formulas for a successful life that can be practiced in your spare time. Don't fall for that stuff, even though crowds of people do. The way to life—to God!—is vigorous and requires total attention.

"Be wary of false preachers who smile a lot, dripping with practiced sincerity. Chances are they are out to rip you off some way or other. Don't be impressed with charisma; look for character. Who preachers *are* is the main thing, not what they say.

"...What is required is serious obedience—*doing* what my Father wills. I can see it now—at the Final Judgment—thousands strutting up to me and saying, 'Master, we preached the Message, we bashed the demons, our God-sponsored projects had everyone talking.' And do you know what I am going to say? 'You missed the boat. All you did was use me to make yourselves important. You don't impress me one bit. You're out of here.'

"...If you work these words into your life, you are like a smart carpenter who built his house on solid rock. Rain poured down, the river flooded, a tornado hit—but nothing moved that house. It was fixed to the rock.

"But if you just use my words in Bible studies and don't work them into your life, you are like a stupid carpenter who built his house on the sandy beach. When a storm rolled in and the waves came up, it collapsed like a house of cards."[109]

When Jesus finished, he let go of a sigh and a radiant smile. I think I sighed and smiled like that once—it was right after giving birth to seven puppies. The crowd heard the sigh. They saw the smile. Then, realizing he was finished, they burst into applause.

"Wow, Jesna! I never heard people clapping for a preacher before. This is more like being at the Super Bowl than being in church."

"You're very right, Pete. You have just heard the greatest sermon that will ever be preached. And everyone here knows that this man, Jesus, is living everything he said. A greater teacher will never be heard in this universe; never will another teacher refer to God as his Father, and be telling the truth."

Jesus Christ, the Son of the living God, sat exhausted on a sparkling rock that he had made a few million years ago, and listened to thousands of his human creations clapping their hands. I think I heard the rock clapping too.

FAMILY DISCUSSION

1. Draw a house built on sand and one built on rock.
2. Tell each other how you plan to make sure you build your house (life) on rock (the words of Jesus' Sermon on the Mount).

SCENE SIXTY-ONE
THE CENTURION OF CAPERNAUM[110]

Jesus got up from his rock and gathered his disciples around. They spoke quietly and then turned and began to walk as a group back down the mountain. Many in the crowd were still applauding as he made his way through their midst. Hundreds squeezed in close enough to pat Jesus on the back or to touch his robe.

The scene, at times, resembled ones I had watched on our TV at home when a rock star, or a famous athlete, is crushed by a herd of humans. Flashing cameras and a band of journalists would have fit right in.

Pete must have had similar thoughts. He said, "Is this where someone asks Jesus where he is going now that he has preached the greatest sermon ever; and he says, 'To Disney World'?"

No one answered, but even Jesna smiled.

It was more than a two-hour walk down the mountain, along the edge of the Sea of Galilee, and back to the village of Capernaum. I was glad we were riding—even though Jesna did manage to hit a few teeth-rattling rocks along the way.

By the time we arrived at Jesus' "home base," the sun was already down for the night and most of the crowd had gone home to bed.

The only lights in town came from a few torches, scattered along the main street. Their battle against the darkness was heroic.

"There he is!" someone shouted from inside the night. "That's

Jesus, there. I'll take you to him." As the voices moved toward us the light began to flicker on their faces.

The man in front was wearing a skirt and vest made of metal. He was also wearing a metal helmet that had two mutton-chop metal sideburns. He was making more noise than a bunch of tin cans banging behind a cat's tail—but the sight wasn't nearly as appealing.

The man in the skirt stopped short in front of Jesus. There was panic on his face. "Master," he said, "my servant is sick. He is paralyzed and in terrible pain. Will you help him?"

The tiredness in Jesus' eyes left immediately. He said, "Yes, I will come and heal him."

But the man answered, "Oh, no! I am not worthy to have you come under my roof; just say the word and my servant will be healed."

With those words, several of the disciples gasped.

"What's going on with them, Jesna?" Mr. Pilgrim asked as he nodded his head in the direction of the gasping and gaping disciples.

"That man is a centurion. He has a hundred soldiers under his command. In essence, he's the Roman military-mayor in charge of this city. He's the most powerful man in town. And he just said he was unworthy to have a homeless Jew come to his house."

"Oh!" said Mr. Pilgrim.

The centurion continued. "I'm a man who takes orders and gives orders. I tell a soldier, 'Go,' and he's gone; to another, 'Come,' and he comes. But if you order the sickness to leave my servant, it will obey you. You are in charge of matters of life."

Jesus seemed totally amazed. For a few seconds he seemed

speechless. Then he said to those who were following him, "I've not yet seen this kind of pure trust in Israel—among the very people who are supposed to know all about God and how he works."

He then turned back to face the centurion and said, "You are the first of many 'outsiders' who will soon be coming from all directions to take their places at God's kingdom banquet. You will sit along with other heroes of faith—Abraham, Isaac, and Jacob—whereas many who grew up hearing about the kingdom, but never entering in through faith, will not be at the table."

"Go," Jesus ordered the centurion. "What you believed could happen already has."

The centurion spun on his heels and bolted away—this time sounding like a box full of empty cans spilling down a flight of stairs.

The next day Capernaum was abuzz. The centurion had returned home to find his paralyzed servant dancing in the front yard. The centurion himself joined in. It was a Jewish folk dance—a real loud one.

FAMILY DISCUSSION

1. Do you know what it means to have faith?

2. Because the centurion had faith, Jesus said he would be remembered with what great men?

3. What seems to be required to be invited to sit at the banquet table in God's kingdom?

SCENE SIXTY-TWO
THE WIDOW'S SON AT NAIN[111]

A few days later Jesus went with his disciples to a small village called Nain. It wasn't too many bumps and bruises for us from Capernaum. We parked the car outside the village and disembarked. Just then, loud shrieks and wails came pouring out through the village gate. We stopped, frozen in our tracks.

As we stood in silence, a procession began to make its way out of the gate. "It's a funeral march," Jesna whispered in a respectful tone.

At the front of the procession several women were crying loudly. They were sobbing with their whole bodies. Behind these women a single woman walked slowly, like a zombie. She was not making a sound, but her grief was the loudest of all.

Behind this woman four men carried what looked like a wooden ladder on their shoulders. On top of that was laid a small bundle of white cloth; it looked like it was wrapped around a child about the size of Pete. A strong scent of spices and flowers issued from the bundle of cloth. Behind these four men dozens of other people walked and sobbed.

One of these said while passing, "I can't believe she lost her only son just months after her husband died."

The other said, "I know, God must really be angry with her."

"So that's somebody's little boy on top of that thing?" Pete asked. And he swallowed hard.

"Yes," Jesna said quietly.

"Is he, uh, is he dead?"

"Yes."

"Do you think he's been dead long?"

"No. It's not like modern funerals. They don't know how to

embalm the body. People are usually buried a few hours after they die."

"You mean that little boy was alive just a few hours ago? This morning?"

"In all likelihood, Pete."

"Look at Jesus!" Priscilla exclaimed. "He's crying."

We all looked. It was obvious that his heart had been broken by what we were seeing. His face was flushed. Both of his cheeks were streaked by tears, and he was breathing in very deeply.

"Wait!" Jesus cried out. But the funeral march continued on. "Don't cry, mother." He said as he walked in a rapid pace to catch up to the men carrying the child. He reached out and touched the wooden bier the boy was laying on. The marchers stopped.

"Young man," Jesus said to the dead child, "I tell you to get up." The boy sat up, like a mummy come back to life. Jesus brushed the cloth back over his head, revealing a pair of darting, brown eyes, enough brown hair for two heads, and the most bewildered face I had ever seen.

Jesus picked up the child (who was probably wondering why so many people had turned out to see him wake up), turned around, and held him out toward his mother. She grabbed him and squeezed him so tightly I thought Jesus might have to bring him back to life again. She cried with deep joy.

The crowd became as quiet as mice. Most dropped to their knees and stared reverently at the ground. Then the one who had said that God must be angry with the woman shouted: "God is back, looking to the needs of his people!"

"He never left," Jesus replied. Then, in a quieter voice, one that only himself and dogs could hear, he said, "and he was never angry at this poor mother."

FAMILY DISCUSSION

1. Why not pause for a few moments and quietly ask, deep inside
   yourself, if any parts of your life have died—or at least become
   weak and ill? Ask Jesus to make this part of you alive and well
   again.

SCENE SIXTY-THREE
ON FOLLOWING JESUS[112]

In a short time we were on the road again—to another village.
Along the way a small crowd had gathered. It marched along
behind and on both sides of us. Jesna kept our car right between
the heels of the disciples and the toes of the followers.
Occasionally someone would step right in the middle of us.
"Hey! Watch that!" Pete would say—still not coming to terms
with being a hologram.

After awhile a man's voice rang out, "Can I come along? I'll
follow you wherever you go!"

Jesus smiled, then said to the man who had run up to his side,
"Are you sure? Foxes have their holes and birds have their nests,
but we don't have a place to stay—not even tonight."

The young man got a serious look on his face and then
dropped back in the pack.

Jesus then turned around, and while walking backwards for a
few paces, looked at another person. "Will you follow me under
those conditions?"

The young man he addressed looked very surprised. But he
managed to stammer out an answer, "Y-Y-Yes, M-Master, I'll follow you. Just let me first go home and make arrangements for my
father's funeral."

"Pssst, Jesna."

"Yes, Pete."

"I thought you said that people were buried within a few hours of dying."

"I did, Pete."

"Well, why does this man say he needs time to make some arrangements?"

"Listen."

Jesus, still walking backwards, had a sly smile on his face as he responded to the man. "Let the dead bury themselves. I want to make you a minister of life, a proclaimer of the kingdom of God."

Within a few moments this man also slowed his pace and dropped further away from the small group of committed disciples and into the crowd of the curious.

Jesus spun back around—facing the future instead of the past. After a few moments passed, a third voice was heard. The words came out wrapped in a proud tone. "I'll go with you Jesus. All I need to do is to say goodbye to my family and get a few things straightened out at home. I can be back in no time. Meet you at the next village."

Jesus stopped. The procession stopped. He turned to face the face that had spoken.

"No procrastination. No backward looks. You can't put God's kingdom off till tomorrow. Seize the day."[113]

FAMILY DISCUSSION

1. Why do you think Jesus wasn't jumping at the chance to add more volunteers?

2. What is there about life in the kingdom that makes it worth
giving up everything for the chance to be a part of it?

SCENE SIXTY-FOUR
STILLING THE STORM[114]

We continued bouncing along behind Jesus and his disciples.
Often the path we were on had enough ruts to make a mountain
goat stumble. The crowd that was following had dropped back a
few steps. I wasn't sure if the increased distance was due to rocks
and gouges in the road or Jesus' penetrating words—about the
cost of being a disciple.

"Jesna."

"Yes, Pete."

"I don't understand something."

"That's why I'm here."

"You would think that Jesus would want to have more people
join him. But it almost seemed like he was trying to chase those
last three away. How come?"

"That's a tough one, Pete. But I'll give you my best shot. Have
you ever seen a picture of the earth, taken from so far out in space
that it looked about the size, well, that the sun does now?"

Pete took a quick peek at the noonday sun and said, "Ouch!
Yes. But it didn't hurt my eyes so bad."

"That's bad-*ly*."

"Oh yeah. Thank-ly, Dad."

Jesna continued, "That view from outer space is a whole different perspective than the one you have right now, isn't it, Pete?"

"Yeah. From here the earth seems humongous. From up there
it seems like a colorful Ping-Pong ball—that you can hide from
your eyes with your thumb."

"Pete, that's what we have to consider when trying to figure out why certain things *seem* to happen the way they do. We see things from up close. God is close too, but he is also so far away that he can view a person's whole life from beginning to end at one time."

"As if it were a Ping-Pong ball?"

"Yes, Pete. As if it were that small. So, to us a stern word or a rejection…"

"Or a spanking?" Pete interrupted.

"Yes, or a spanking, these things can seem very big to us. They make God seem cruel for being part of it. But from his perspective, because he can see the course of a whole life, because he knows which events will help people choose a different course, the picture may look very different.

"So Pete, while we will never have his view-from-way-above perspective, we know enough about his love for us, and for those three men he confronted about wanting to follow him, we can accept that concern was for the course of their whole life, and not just that one moment.

"When they want to follow him for all the right reasons, and know the score, I am sure they'll be welcomed with a bear hug. And I am doubly sure that what he just said to them will increase and not decrease the chances of that happening."

Pete was slowly nodding his head. He seemed satisfied with Jesna's answer. Jesus was smiling. He seemed satisfied, too.

Later that day we arrived at the shore of the Sea of Galilee. A single boat was tied to a tree on the bank by a thick, hairy rope.

Jesus walked over to a man sitting by the tree. The old man looked tired, perhaps from a hard day's fishing. Jesus spoke a few words and the man quickly nodded "yes." The man stood to his feet, untied a knot in the rope and handed it to Jesus. Jesus handed him a coin and said, "Thank you. Your boat will be back tomorrow."

As the crowd watched from the shore, Jesus and the disciples piled into the boat. Peter took the lead in getting it seaworthy.

"Fly or float?" Jesna asked as she began to punch buttons on the dash of our car.

"Huh?" said the Pilgrims.

"Fly or float? We're going to follow them out into the lake. Do you want to fly overhead or float along beside?"

"Oh, let's float," Pete said. "We haven't done that yet." The other four nodded their agreement.

Jesna then pressed two bright red buttons and pulled down on a lever and we drove right out onto the water.

"I don't believe it!" shouted Pete. "This car is ambidextrous!"

"That's 'amphibious,' Pete. Amphibious. Like a frog."

"OK, OK, Priscilla. That's what I meant. It's a frogmobile. And I wouldn't be surprised if it started catching flies for fuel."

Three of the disciples were waist-deep in water and were shoving the boat away from shore. It took most of the rest of the disciples to hoist them aboard.

With Jesna at the helm, we floated alongside, about one good flying-fish jump away. A bobbing crowd waved from the shore.

After a few minutes Pete asked, "Where's Jesus wanting to go?"

"Look," Jesna answered. "He's already there."

We all looked and saw that Jesus was curled around a cushion at the back of the boat, fast asleep.

For the next couple of hours we floated together. The disciples were letting their big wooden boat drift with the currents as they laughed and talked with each other. They all seemed right at home, except maybe Matthew, the tax collector. He looked a little green.

As time passed the wind began to pick up some speed—a lot of speed—and the sky became dark with dirty-gray clouds.

"Hey!" Pete said, "where did the sun go? I don't like the looks of this."

It wasn't long until both boats began to be tossed around by giant, watery hands. Lightning started shooting jagged lines across the sky, and thunder roared with the deepest voice I had ever heard.

The disciples' faces had become ghostly white against the dark background (except for Matthew's, which was a deeper shade of green).

The Pilgrims had death grips on the sides of our car-boat. They looked as if they expected to become ghosts with the next crashing wave. "I want to go HOOOOME!!!" Pete screamed. I was getting bounced around a bit, but it was kind of fun.

Only Jesna and Jesus were calm. In fact, Jesus was still asleep.

As both boats were being swamped with water, one of the disciples cried out to Jesus, "Master! Don't you care that we are about to die?"

Jesus woke up. He looked around from his position as a passenger in the last car on a roller coaster. Then he said, as he yawned and scratched his head, "You woke me up for this? Where is your faith today, fellahs?"

Then he stood and looked out at the angry sky and the raging sea and he shouted, "Be silent!"

And immediately the winds ceased. Within moments the waves unrolled and the sea became smooth as glass. The clouds parted overhead, exiting to the left and right.

Both boats were motionless. The only movement was that of slow-growing shadows cast by a warm, late-afternoon sun. The Son of God lay back down. He wanted to finish his nap. Who was going to stop him?

FAMILY DISCUSSION

1. If you were going to ask Jesus to still a storm in your life, what would it be?

2. Are you ready to do that now?

SCENE SIXTY-FIVE
JESUS AND THE WILD MAN[115]

We spent the night at sea. As the sun arrived the next morning, so did we—on the other side of the Sea of Galilee, in the country of Gadara.

Jesna told us that we were on the southeastern shore of the huge sea, "about as far away from Capernaum as you can get and still dangle your feet in the same lake."

Looking up from where we floated, brown, mostly barren hills tumbled down to meet us. There were plenty of rocks and sand but trees and plants were scarce.

Jesus and some of the disciples piled out of their boat and into the shallow water as Simon Peter anchored the vessel to a giant piece of driftwood.

Then we heard it—a blood-curdling scream. We looked up and saw a scene from a horror movie, running right for us. A man (I think it was a man—smelled a little bit like men) was running and screaming his way toward us from about two hundred feet away.

Broken chains clanked from his ankles as he ran toward us in a side-to-side gait—150 feet and closing. Frayed ropes were tied to his waist and neck and floated behind him like empty kite strings—100 feet. His clothes were dirty rags, his hair was matted wool, and his body was covered with hundreds of wounds, most still bleeding—50 feet. His teeth were yellow; his eyes were wild animals. He beat two jagged rocks together as he ran. The Pilgrims grabbed each other and tried to make a human fort—10 feet. I growled and then barked. I just couldn't help it, I was so scared.

"Come out of him!" Jesus shouted.

The hideous creature collapsed at the feet of Jesus like a crumpled sail.

The man raised his body as if he were doing a push-up, arched his back, and looked Jesus in the face, and then quickly looked away from Jesus' face as he snarled in a loud, gargling voice,

"What business do you have, Jesus, Son of the High God, messing with me? I swear to God, don't give me a hard time!"[116]

Jesus asked the man to tell his name.

"My name is Legion; for we are many in here."

Then in the pitiful, high-pitched voice he begged, "Don't make us leave this country."

The man looked back over his right shoulder. He appeared to be gazing at a herd of pigs that was rooting in the dirt on a nearby hillside. "Send us to the pigs, so we can live in them."

"So be it. Go!" Jesus said in the same tone of voice he used to address the storm.

The man crumpled face first into the sand. His body seemed totally relaxed, limp.

The pigs were not so fortunate. They began to squeal as if they were being branded with a thousand hot pokers. Some reared back on their hind hooves and kicked at the air like wild horses. Then in a cloud of dust, they were off. They stampeded over the edge of a cliff, fell into the lake, and were drowned.

Jesus and the disciples tended to the man who lay before them just as the angels had nursed Jesus after his time in the wilderness.

When an angry band of people from town arrived—to rebuke whoever was responsible for the death of the pig herd—they saw the "madman" sitting with Jesus and the disciples. He was wearing clean clothes (some of Jesus' friends were wearing less), and was talking rationally in a normal, human voice.

It was obvious that the townsfolk were amazed. They were in awe. But their anger over the lost pigs called attention to itself. "But what about our pigs! What happened to them?"

"I think they committed 'Soo-eee side,'" Pete giggled before his father could silence him with a stern look.

"Who's going to pay for the pigs?" another shouted.

The crowd demanded that Jesus leave and not come back.

As Jesus and the disciples were getting back into the boat, the demon-freed man grabbed Jesus by the arm and asked if he could come, too.

Jesus smiled at him with the warmth of a dozen suns and said, "No, not now. Go home and tell your people what has happened. Tell them that you have been set free by love."

With the man waving goodbye from the shore, Jesna said, "That man becomes one of the best evangelists this area will ever know."

"And I bet he stays away from ham sandwiches, too," Pete added.

FAMILY DISCUSSION

1. What was it that came out of the man and went into the pigs?

2. What happened to the man when the demons came out?

3. What did the man become? What does it mean to be an evangelist?

SCENE SIXTY-SIX
THE WOMAN WITH A HEMORRHAGE[117]

Jesus and the disciples traveled back across the Sea of Galilee, against the wind. This time it took a lot more elbow grease. They were rowing against a wind that just an hour earlier had been their friend. Bread, dates, and cheese fueled them for the journey.

Before the sun set, they returned the boat to the old fisherman. Jesus offered him all the food they had not eaten as payment for his inconvenience. He waved the gift away with his face and hands. "I am honored to be able to say that you once sat in my humble boat," he said. Jesus smiled and honored him further with a hug.

To everyone's apparent surprise a crowd was still waiting by the seaside. In fact, it had grown.

As Jesus turned away from the fisherman, a man came running through the crowd, gold chains bouncing around his neck, and fell to his knees at Jesus' feet. He was almost hysterical as he begged, "My precious daughter, my only daughter, is about to die. Please, I beg you, come and lay hands on her so she will get well and live!"

The frantic man was wearing fine new robes and he smelled of incense—like the kind I had enjoyed in the synagogue in Capernaum.

"That's Jairus," Jesna said. "He's one of the rulers of the synagogue."

"I thought I recognized him," Pete said.

Jesna continued, "If he's asking for Jesus' help, you can be sure he is desperate—and that he has tried everything else first. He could lose his position in the church for this kind of public display."

"What do you mean?" Priscilla asked.

"He's a keeper of the old system, the old ways of believing. Jesus is a teacher of a whole new way of thinking and living. The Pharisees, the Sadducees (mostly priests and their families), and men like Jairus (elected leaders in the church) feel threatened by someone proposing a 'new way.' It's the 'old way' that's provided their preferred positions in life."

As Jesna finished talking, Jesus was placing his arm around Jairus' back and leading him back through the middle of the large crowd toward Capernaum.

Jesna converted our "frogmobile" back into a Land Rover and we bounced along behind.

Before we had gone two hundred yards, we saw a very strange sight. A woman with a robe and feet streaked by dull red stains came up behind the crowd that had formed a tight semicircle behind Jesus and Jairus.

She seemed very weak, but was desperately trying to get a hand in, through, over, or around the crowd—toward Jesus.

"What's that woman doing?" Pete asked. "Is she trying to grab Jesus?"

Before Jesna could answer, the crowd stopped moving forward, and Jesus said in a clear voice, "Who touched my robe?"

One of his disciples answered for the crowd. "What are you talking about? With this crowd pushing and jostling you, it could have been anybody. It probably was everybody."

But Jesus paid no attention to the question from his friend. He knew something the disciple did not. He looked around into the faces of the crowd, searching for the answer.

The woman spoke up. She was trembling like a puppy on a cold day in January. "It was me. I touched you," she confessed.

"Why?" Jesus asked.

"Because, for twelve years I have been sick. I've been bleeding and it has not stopped. I've seen every physician in Galilee. They took my money and they left me poor and still sick. Today I said to myself, *If I can just touch Jesus' robe—just a touch—I'll be healed.*

"When I touched you," she continued, "I felt tingling energy surging throughout my body. And I am healed! I'm sorry."

"I am delighted!" Jesus beamed. "I felt your faith touch me, too. And I felt healing energy leaving me.

"Daughter, you took a risk of faith, and now you're healed and whole. Live well, live blessed! Be healed of your plague."[118]

FAMILY DISCUSSION

1. What do you think Jesus and the woman felt when faith and healing were shooting back and forth between them?

2. If you could touch Jesus right now, what would your touch be asking to receive?

SCENE SIXTY-SEVEN
JAIRUS' DAUGHTER[119]

"No! Noooo!" Jairus screamed at heart-stopping volume and collapsed on the ground, clawing at this robe and tearing it.

"What's going on?" Pete asked.

"Look, coming there," Jesna answered, "those men are from Jairus' house. Their clothes are torn from their necks to the center of their chests. It looks like Jairus' daughter is dead."

A man from the approaching group spoke with despair. "Jairus, your daughter is dead. There's no need to bother this *teacher* anymore." He shot a sarcastic sneer at Jesus. "He can't help you."

As Jairus' "friends" were pulling him to his feet, Jesus spoke.

"Don't listen to them, Jairus. Trust me. Like she did," and he pointed to the smiling woman.

"Yes!" the woman said. "Trust the Healer."

Jairus withdrew his arms from those of his friends and grabbed the arm of Jesus. "Please. Come to my house and heal my daughter."

"She's dead!" his friends said. Then one of them pulled at his robe causing the tear in his robe to grow. "DEAD!"

Jairus pushed his friend aside like a man flinging back a saloon door, grabbed Jesus by the hand, and continued on. We drove behind them, with the disciples and most of the crowd quick-stepping to keep up.

When we arrived at Jairus' house, what greeted us was chilling. We were met by waves of sound—the tearing of garments, wailing shrieks, and the eerie song of a dozen sad flutes. When the people saw Jairus, the volume of both tears and wails increased dramatically. Jairus' house was a sea of loud, anguished pandemonium.

Jesus waded through the courtyard and front room of the house. Then, before entering the back room where the child lay, he turned and spoke to the noisy crowd. "Why do you make a tumult and weep? The child is not dead but sleeping."[120]

The crowd instantly became hostile and jeered at Jesus. "You're a madman!" "Have you no respect for the dead?" "For the parents of the dead?" "Get out!"

Jesus addressed them as he had the violent storm of the night before, like the turbulent storm they were. "Leave! Now!"

He took Jairus and the child's mother into the room where their daughter lay still, pale, and cold.

The room was silent except for the sounds from the sandals of mourners stomping out of the house. He waited a few seconds. It was quiet.

Then he took the child by the hand and said in a quiet, calm voice, *"Talitha cumi."*

"What did he say?" Pete asked.

"That means, 'Little girl, get up' in their language."

The child's eyes opened slowly and grew very wide. Her

parents exploded with joy. Their smiling faces shone. The little girl, who looked to be about Priscilla's age, swung her feet over the side of the bed and stood up.

"She's probably very hungry," Jesus said as he touched the child's hair. "If I were you, I'd fix her favorite meal."

He turned and left with the secrecy of the Lone Ranger. Twelve "Tontos" followed behind, shaking their heads in obvious awe of the unmasked Healer.

FAMILY DISCUSSION

1. Do you think the young girl was really dead?
2. Imagine yourself present with the Jairus' for dinner that evening. What do you think they talked about?
3. How does this story make you feel about the power of Jesus?

SCENE SIXTY-EIGHT
THE DUMB DEMONIAC[121]

Jesus walked back out of Jairus' house with us and the disciples close on his heels. As he passed through the courtyard gate, a loudmouthed man with sort of a pillow case strapped to his head hollered at Jesus, "Done so soon, healer? Let that be a lesson to you. Keep your nose out of other peoples' affairs!"

Jesus didn't tell the man what had happened in the back room of the house. He just nodded a "thank you" and kept walking.

Pete was not so kind, however. "You... you. If you had half the sense God gave a flea you'd be kissing Jesus' feet instead of mocking him. If he can raise 'em up, he can knock 'em dead. He is the Son of God, ya know."

"Who told you Jesus is the 'Son of God?'" Jesna asked Pete.

"Why *you* did, Jesna. About a million times."

"But," she said, "when did you start to believe it for yourself?"

"Aw, come on, Jesna. Raising people from the dead. Telling storms to shut their faces. Turning water into wine. I mean, nobody else could do that stuff. I wouldn't be surprised if he started walking on water any minute now. I mean, who else could he be?"

Jesna smiled a very satisfied smile. Mr. Pilgrim seemed lost in the thoughts Pete had set in motion.

Before Jesus had put twenty paces between himself and his verbal assassin, a man came running up to him. He was leading another man by the hand as if he were a pet monkey.

"Jesus! You must help my friend. He's been struck dumb by an evil spirit. He's been unable to talk for more than a month. All he can do now is growl and hiss."

Jesus turned and faced both men. One was standing tall, looking Jesus squarely in the eye. The other was hunched over. His left arm hung limp toward the ground like a broken chime; his right hand was held by his friend. The animal-man was drooling at the mouth. His eyes were glazed. When Jesus' eyes found his, he quickly turned his head and began making deep gargling sounds in his throat.

"See! See!" His keeper said. "He used to be able to talk. He had a job. He *has* a wife and children. Please, please, help him. I know you can."

Jesus looked at the tormented man and simply said, "Be gone!"

Immediately the man straightened his posture, squared his shoulders, and began to speak in a clear voice. The one who had brought him to Jesus fell to his knees and closed his eyes. His lips moved with prayer. The crowd—many of whom had been mourners at Jairus' house—broke out in spontaneous applause that became a choir of "Wow!" and "Did you see that!" There was one noticeable mute in the ensemble.

The man who had so harshly criticized Jesus walked over and began to whisper with three black-robed Pharisees. In a few moments one of the men in black spoke. "This is all just a bunch of hocus pocus. Pointing to Jesus, he declared, "If that man has any power it's because he's made a pact with the Devil!"

This outburst silenced the chorus and started a low murmur in the crowd. Then, several heads began nodding in agreement. Jesus made no effort to put the record straight. He kissed the delivered man on the cheek, turned, and continued to walk away.

"Thank you, Son of God!" said the healed one. In contrast to the crowd, he was neither dumb nor mute.

FAMILY DISCUSSION

1. If you were present with the Pilgrims, would you agree with Pete that Jesus is God's Son?

2. What makes you believe that?

SCENE SIXTY-NINE
THE HARVEST IS GREAT[122]

Jesus kept walking until the sun set and Capernaum had turned into a round mound of little lights, sparkling dimly in the distance. For the next several weeks we drove along behind Jesus and the disciples as they traveled to many of the small villages that hugged the shoreline of the Sea of Galilee.

The landscape around the lake was beautiful. We wandered over gentle, green hills and around, and through, dozens of flocks of sheep. Fishing boats plied the water. The odors of fish and sheep were never out of range of my eager nose.

More than once Jesna commented how she thought the scenery around Galilee must be a lot like that of Eden. It certainly stood in contrast to the barren, lifeless, Judean wilderness to the south. Every blade of grass that had been there had moved north a long time ago.

The beauty of the landscape also stood in contrast to the plainness, the ugliness, in fact, of most of the people who came out to hear Jesus talk about life in his Father's kingdom. While the crowds would be dotted with a few "beautiful" people in clean, brightly colored robes, with washed faces and scented hair, most of the people were broken and twisted with gaptoothed smiles and deep-set eyes.

But when Jesus talked about God's love, untwisted their limbs, touched them with his hand or a smile, the ugliest of the broken people beamed with more loveliness than a sunset on the lake.

One evening, at sunset, Jesus was preaching to a large crowd by the sea shore. His words were riding on a gentle breeze. The golden rays of the half-set sun were glowing behind Jesus, painting the dirty, brown faces in the crowd with orange. Jesus finished a paragraph and stopped talking. His voice broke with emotion as he looked out over the people.

He turned to his band of disciples and seemed to be trying very hard not to cry, when he said, "Look at all these, so confused and aimless, like sheep without a shepherd.

"Look," he said again, "do you see what I see? What a beautiful field of wheat they are! What a rich and bountiful harvest! Pray with me now that our Father will send more shepherds and more harvesters."

Jesus and the disciples bowed and prayed. A thousand human grainstalks rippled with bowing heads. Four of them belonged to the Pilgrims.

FAMILY DISCUSSION

1. Why do you think Jesus' message appealed more to the poor and common than the rich and famous?

2. Why do you think Jesus was crying?

SCENE SEVENTY
THE FATE OF THE DISCIPLES[123]

Before there was time to unbow a head, Simon Peter began tugging on the sleeve of Jesus' robe.

"Jesus!" he said excitedly.

"What is it, Peter?"

"We'll be your harvesters!" he said as he glanced around at the others. Their heads began to rapidly nod in agreement. "We've been watching and learning from you. Say the word and we will try to do the things that you have done."

"Have you learned enough to know that there is nothing you can do in your own power to help these people? Have you learned that all power, all love, all help, and healing come through my Father?"

They all nodded again, but less vigorously this time.

"Then," Jesus said in a much louder voice, "I commission you twelve as official harvesters. You, through God your Father, will have power over unclean spirits. You will be able to call on God's mercy for the healing of broken bodies and minds."

The crowd erupted with applause. But Jesus was not finished. He not only gave them a commission but also a charge:

"Don't begin by traveling to some faroff place to convert unbelievers. And don't try to be dramatic by tackling some public enemy. Go to the lost, confused people right here in the neighborhood. Tell them that the kingdom is here. Bring health to the sick. Raise the dead. Touch the untouchables. Kick out the demons. You have been treated generously, so live generously.

"...When you enter a town or village, don't insist on staying in a luxury inn. Get a modest place with some modest people, and be content there until you leave.

"...Don't be naive. Some people will impugn your motives, others will smear your reputation—just because you believe in me. Don't be upset when they haul you before the civil authorities. Without knowing it, they've done you—and me—a favor, given you a platform for preaching the kingdom news!... The right words will be there; the Spirit of your Father will supply the words.

"When people realize it is the living God you are presenting and not some idol that makes them feel good, they are going to turn on you, even people in your own family. There is a great irony here: proclaiming so much love, experiencing so much hate! But don't quit. Don't cave in. It is well worth it in the end.

"...A student doesn't get a better desk than her teacher. A laborer doesn't make more money than his boss. Be content—pleased, even—when you, my students, my harvest hands, get the same treatment I get. If they call me, the Master, 'Dung-face,' what can the workers expect?"[124]

"Jesus."

Neither the crowd, nor the disciples, could see that it was now Pete—not Peter—who was tugging on Jesus' robe.

"Yes, Pete," Jesus said with a warm smile, "what is it you want?"

"I'd like to work on your farm, too."

To everyone but me, the Pilgrims, and Jesna, it looked like Jesus was hugging the air.

FAMILY DISCUSSION

1. Do you think it was hard for the disciples to do what Jesus did?

2. What would you do if you heard Jesus asking you to do what he told his disciples to do?

SCENE SEVENTY-ONE
SPEAK UP, DON'T BE AFRAID[125]

With Pete and Jesus standing arm in arm, Jesus turned his focus back to his disciples. The multitude was still listening as if he were talking to them—perhaps he was.

"So as you go out... Don't be bluffed into silence by the threats of bullies. There's nothing they can do to your soul, your core being. Save your fear for God, who holds your entire life—body and soul—in his hands.

"What's the price of a pet canary? Some loose change, right? And God cares what happens to it even more than you do. He pays even greater attention to you, down to the last detail— even numbering the hairs on your head! So don't be intimidated by all this bully talk. You're worth more than a million canaries."[126]

"Wait a minute! Wait a minute, Jesna!" Priscilla said in a demanding voice. "I can't quite get this figured out. In one sentence he's telling the disciples not to be afraid. Then in the very next one he's saying they should be afraid of God."

"So what do you not understand, Priscilla?"

"I read somewhere," Priscilla explained, "that fear and love are exact opposites. A person can't be afraid and in love at the exact same time. It would be like trying to be down and up at the same time."

"I'm still not sure what you can't figure out," Jesna said.

"Jesus just told his disciples to fear God. But he's said a bunch more times to love God. How can you do both—at the same time?"

"Oh, I see," Jesna said. "Jesus said to not be afraid of bullies, right?"

"Yeah, because they can't hurt the part of you that really matters, that lasts forever—your soul."

"Yes, Priscilla, that's right. Then he said that if you are going to be afraid of anyone, be afraid of God, because he can affect what happens to your soul."

"Sooo, he said to be afraid of God, but we're supposed to be in love with God."

"That's right, Priscilla. The only thing to be afraid of in the entire universe loves you—loves you more than a million canaries, so much that he keeps up with the number of hairs on your head."

"So it sounds like there really isn't anything to be afraid of?"

"Only that you might start believing the lies of Satan and forget to be in awe of God. If that happened you might decide to leave the Father's kingdom."

"Oh. What would happen then?"

"He'd walk to the very edge of his kingdom every morning and wait for you to come back."

"What if you didn't come back?"

"He'd send his Boy, Jesus, to go find you."

"Then," Priscilla said, "there is nothing to be afraid of?"

"Well, Priscilla, you can see how much Jesus loves these people. You know what he gave up in heaven to be down here with them. But you haven't seen him pick somebody up and drag him, kicking and screaming, off to heaven."

"No, I haven't seen that."

"Then you should be afraid."

"Huh?"

"Afraid that you might underestimate the power of God's love and refuse to follow it back home. That's a pretty scary thought. But if you stay in awe of God, realizing that it is he, and only he, who determines the fate of your soul, you will be afraid, afraid of being away from his love. And you'll come back home where he can turn your fear inside out. And you already know that inside out fear is love."

FAMILY DISCUSSION

1. What do you think Proverbs 9:10 means? That "The fear of the Lord is the beginning of wisdom and the knowledge of the Holy *is* understanding" (KJV).

2. What part of us can our enemy Satan not touch because we belong to God?

SCENE SEVENTY-TWO
THE CONDITIONS AND REWARDS OF DISCIPLESHIP[127]

Jesus continued instructing his disciples with his littlest pupil, Pete, still tucked in at his side. The open arms of the Sea of Galilee were the backdrop for his teaching.

"If you don't go all the way with me, through thick and thin, you don't deserve me. If your first concern is to look after yourself, you'll never find yourself. But if you forget about yourself [even to the point of great personal pain] and look to me, you'll find both yourself and me."[128]

"OK, Jesna. My turn."

"I thought that might get your attention, Mr. Pilgrim."

"Well, yes, it did. I've been listening very carefully these past thirty-one years…"

"It's only been about fifty-five seconds of real time, Dad."

"Thanks, Priscilla," Mr. Pilgrim said as he rolled his eyes to the east. "I've been listening and I'm convinced that Jesus is the wisest man that I've ever heard. But how can he expect me to both find myself and lose myself? A penny can't be both found and lost at the same time."

"Certainly, Mr. Pilgrim, Jesus is the wisest man you have ever met. He's also the only God you will *ever* meet. And as God, he knows something you don't. You have two pennies. Not just one."

"What's that?"

"There are two of you, of anyone. You have a 'me-self' and a 'we-self' under your skin."

"Still not with you."

"It goes back to your great, great, great, great grandparents, Adam and Eve, Mr. Pilgrim. When they 'fell' (failed) in the Garden of Eden, they kept on falling. They fell so far that they ended up a long way from their truest selves—the self God had created. It's that self that loves God and his creation. It's that self I am calling the 'we-self.' It's the one that can actually obey the 'Golden Rule' and keep the commandment to love, because it thinks more about 'we' than 'me.'

"To be set free to live in God's kingdom means that the fallen 'we-self' has to get back up and get back behind the steering wheel of your life.

"That's what Jesus means by 'forgetting yourself' (your 'me-self,' your selfish nature) to 'find yourself' (your 'we-self,' the self that thinks about others), and he's the only one that can help you make it happen.

"He's saying that to do this, you'll have to be willing to let go of everything but your love and trust in him. It's sort of like a death. It is a death of selfishness, and it can be really painful."

"So," Pete smiled at us from under Jesus' arm. "Jesus, here, wants us to be like the three little pigs, and go 'We, We, We. All the way back home.'"

Jesna barked out a laugh that a Great Dane would be proud of. "That's better than I can say it, Pete. Yes, all the way to your true home."

FAMILY DISCUSSION

1. What does it mean to "forget yourself"?

2. When we forget ourselves, how do we treat others?

3. What are some good ways to forget self and love others?

SCENE SEVENTY-THREE
JOHN THE BAPTIST'S QUESTION[129]

"Back in the car!" Jesna shouted. "It's time for a trip."

From Jesus' side and from all directions we found our way back to the car. Pete dove in, head first. His feet were still dangling where his arms should have been when Jesna punched the last button and sent us airborne. It just about made me swallow my tongue which had been hanging out as I panted. When Pete had righted himself we were right at one hundred feet and climbing.

"Where are we going in such a hurry, Jesna?" Pete asked as he shook some dead grass that had been on the floor board from his hair.

"We're going to the dungeon at Herod's palace. John's disciples are already there, about to speak with him."

"You can let me off right here," Pete suggested. "I'm not real big into dungeons. The door could lock behind us, ya know."

"Think again, little brother. That first step is about two hundred feet straight down."

"Whoa," Pete gasped. "Why are those ants down there wearing bathrobes?"

"Those aren't…" Priscilla punched him.

"I know. I know."

I decided I didn't want to sit between those two if they were going to keep punching each other.

"Jesna."

"Yes, Mrs. Pilgrim."

"Who is the 'John' that's in the dungeon? The one who baptized Jesus out in the wilderness?"

"That's right. John the Baptist, Jesus' cousin. He's been held by Herod for the last seven months. Herod is allowing two of his disciples to visit him today. Ooops! Hold on! Here we are!"

With that the bottom fell out of the ride and my stomach came to the top of my throat. As we plummeted straight for a huge rock building, everyone's hair stood to attention, cheeks ballooned with air, and nostrils became round Os—like a pig's. Just before the ground leapt up into our faces, we leveled off and began bursting through thick stone walls.

"YYYyyyoooooaaaaaahh!" sang a quartet of Pilgrims. It was a long time since we had flown through a building.

We flew through rooms full of big wooden furniture and colorful tapestries as Jesna pumped the brakes. Then, just a few feet from a round man, we came to a stop. The man, who sat gnawing on two fists full of mutton, couldn't see us; and he certainly couldn't hear us over all the lip-smacking.

Jesna pulled back on a lever and we began to sink through the floor. "Hey! Save me some of that, uh, whatever it is," Pete shouted as the floor was becoming our new ceiling.

We continued our descent. "All out for Roman antiques," Pete giggled.

When our elevator finally came to a stop, there was no doubt about which floor we were on. It was the basement of a dungeon.

"Don't get out," Jesna whispered.

"Don't worry," said Priscilla, "I wouldn't want my garbage to get out here."

We were in the bowels of Herod's castle. The light from a single torch was all that kept us from drowning in darkness. It cast flickering light on moist rock walls and on the backs of two men who were huddled by a wooden door about thirty feet away.

Driving through ankle-deep water, we inched toward the men. The air was thick with the smell of decay, moldiness, and lots of other icky stuff. My nose twitched. I thought I was going to sneeze.

"Look! Listen!" Jesna said.

"Oh, my goodness!" cried Mrs. Pilgrim. "Is that John the Baptist?"

"Yes."

John's face was barely recognizable as it peered out from between two iron bars of a window in the door to his cell.

It seemed that he had aged twenty years during the past seven months; but it was hard to tell what was underneath the thick coat of grime he now wore.

You could tell he was glad to see his friends. That was obvious from the smile in his eyes and clean streaks beneath them. Finally, we were close enough to hear him speak.

"Word about Jesus has seeped in here, right under Herod's fat nose. It seems that he really is 'the One.' But I must know for sure. Go ask him for me, 'Are you the One who is to come, or should we look for another?'"

Then John coughed a deep, hacking cough. A trio of guards made a quick entrance, grabbed his disciples by their arms and started pulling them away.

"John," Pete whispered, when the guards were gone. "He's the One, all right. You did your job real good. Now he's doing his."

But John was a man. He couldn't hear Pete's voice.

FAMILY DISCUSSION

1. Can you imagine what life was like for John the Baptist during those seven months in Herod's prison?

2. Do you think that being in a dungeon so long made him lose his confidence?

3. What is the last hardship you've experienced that's made it difficult for you to hold on to your faith in God?

SCENE SEVENTY-FOUR
JESUS ANSWERS JOHN'S MESSENGERS[130]

Jesna began to play the panel of buttons as if they were keys on a piano. Within seconds Herod's dungeon was spinning around us in dark swatches and circular streaks of light.

"Will we see poor John again?" Pete asked from the eye of the storm.

"You'll see him again, Pete, but I don't think you want to know about that right now."

Suddenly the spin cycle became very bright. The change was so abrupt it was painful and caused us all to squint tightly. The brightness lasted for several seconds; then all the whirling stopped. After our eyeballs made a few more laps around the inside of our heads and our pupils reopened for business, we could see that we were back out in the Galilean countryside, on the shore of Jesus' favorite lake.

Jesus was standing before another crowd. It didn't take long to tell that he was talking about his choice topic—life in his Father's kingdom.

"Look," said Jesna. "Recognize them?"

Two men were approaching from the north. They had a rough and rugged look and the smell of stale camel skins.

"No. Who are they?" Pete asked.

"Oh, that's right," Jesna answered. "They had their backs to you before. It's John's disciples. They've been on the road for several days, since leaving the dungeon."

"I don't like to think about John still in that dark place," Mrs. Pilgrim said.

"Me neither, Mom," Priscilla and Pete said together.

Mr. Pilgrim just shuddered and I twitched my nose again.

"Jesus!" one of the men called out while Jesus was in the middle of a sentence. Jesus left his sentence half-constructed and turned to see who had called his name.

"Jesus," John's disciple continued, "we've just come from our master, John the Baptist." Jesus' face broke into a smile.

"And he want's to know if you are the One we've been expecting, or are we still waiting?"

Jesus kept smiling, but a sad look drifted across his eyes.

"Have a seat," Jesus said. "Watch and listen for a while. Then you can tell me if I am the One."

A couple of hours passed. In that time Jesus finished his teaching. There were lots of stories.

When the last was told a line of people emerged from the crowd and stretched its way down to where Jesus stood. He handed out miracles to everyone in line. They were as plentiful as candy at a Christmas parade.

When the last person in line had been touched by Jesus he turned to John's two followers and spoke. "Go and tell my poor friend, John, what you have just seen and heard:

> "The blind see,
> The lame walk,
> Lepers are cleansed,
> The deaf hear,
> The dead are raised,
> The wretched of the earth have God's
> salvation hospitality extended to them."[131]

John's messengers slowly stood to their feet. They gave Jesus a reverent nod and began to retrace their steps.

"And tell him I'm grateful. He prepared the way for all that has happened," Jesus called to the backs of the two men.

He then turned back to the crowd of kingdom beneficiaries and said, "I tell you the truth: of all born on earth none is greater than John; yet" (and he paused for several seconds) "the least person in the kingdom of God is greater than he. My Father's kingdom is that much greater than is any dominion here on earth."

FAMILY DISCUSSION

1. Why didn't Jesus just tell John's disciples what they wanted to know? Why did he make them wait and watch?

2. How can it be that the "least in the Kingdom of Heaven" is greater than the messenger of Jesus, John the Baptist?

SCENE SEVENTY-FIVE
"COME UNTO ME"[132]

Jesus continued teaching as John's disciples grew smaller and smaller in the distance. The crowd was all ears. After all, most had just received a miracle from the teacher. About the time that the two messengers disappeared over the horizon, Jesus said:

"Any of you who is weary with a heavy burden, come to me and you will receive rest. Take my yoke. Put it on and learn from me; I am gentle and meek, you will find rest for your souls as you walk by my side. You will find that my yoke is easy and my burden for you is light."[133]

"Wait a minute. Wait a minute," Pete said. "What did he just say? I was daydreaming, but I thought he said something about yolks being greasy if you have them over light. Is he taking orders? Because if he is..."

"He SAID, little brother, 'My yoke is easy and my burden for you is light.'"

"Well, what in the world does that mean?"

"Yokes are very interesting, Pete," Jesna inserted. "Do any of you know what they are?"

Only Mr. and Mrs. Pilgrim nodded, "Yes."

"A yoke is a carved bar of wood that is put around the necks of animals (usually oxen) so that they can pull together in doing a job—like plowing a field. It's like a large wooden collar-for-two, with leather straps or ropes that connect it to something—like a plow."

"So," Pete said, "it's a way to make a two-horse power, I mean, a two-ox-powered motor."

"That's right. And, two oxen yoked together can do a lot more work in a day than just one. Two yoked oxen can plow about an acre of land in one day."

"But Jesna," Priscilla said, "Doesn't that hurt their necks—to be wearing a wooden collar?"

"Yokes are very carefully carved to fit the neck of the animal that will be wearing it."

"You mean, Jesna," Pete interrupted, "they have wood tailors that come out and measure cows' necks?"

"Oxen, Pete. But yes, they do have yoke tailors. Jesus was a carpenter, you know, I imagine he's been a yoke tailor a few times in the past."

A few seconds passed before Jesna spoke again.

"You look troubled, Mr. Pilgrim. What is it?"

"I am troubled. At least confused. Jesus said he is offering an 'easy' yoke and a 'light' burden. But I can't see what would be easy about pulling a plow all day."

"I understand, Mr. Pilgrim. I thought you might even be about to ask about John the Baptist and whether or not he feels like he has a light burden right now."

"Well, yes, that thought did cross my mind."

"I think," Jesna continued, "Jesus is saying a couple of things that are really, really important. First, he's probably referring to the heavy religious burden that the Pharisees would put on the people. He's saying his way is a way of freedom—being with God and your neighbor, loving them, walking with them. The Pharisees' way is a heavy ordeal of ill-fitting rules and regulations.

"But I think he's saying something far more

important than that. He's offering an invitation to come and hitch your plow to his team, so to speak. Keep company with Jesus; be connected to him by a beam of love, and he'll walk beside you and teach you how to live—while he helps you pull your load."

"Wow!" Pete exclaimed. "That's like being able to hook your yoke to a two-ton, turbo-charged tractor."

"You're some theologian, Pete," Jesna giggled, until she saw Mr. Pilgrim's stone face.

"But what about John?" the stone spoke.

"Being a believer in Christ Jesus doesn't mean that there's no burden behind you. It just means that you are yoked together to a loving Friend, who just happens to be like a two-ton tractor.

"When you saw John in prison he was very discouraged. And he had 'unhooked' himself from the yoke he had shared with God. He was trying to pull his huge burden all alone. That's why he sent his friends to Jesus. But when he hears what his two messengers have to say, he'll be putting his yoke back on, and God will pull him all the way home."

Jesna stopped talking and Jesus' words immediately filled the silent space.

"Keep company with me and you'll learn to live freely and lightly."[134]

Mr. Pilgrim's face cracked with a warm smile.

FAMILY DISCUSSION

1. What are the advantages of being "yoked" to God and letting him help you as you go through life?

2. What do you think the saying means "A burden shared is cut in half, but a joy shared doubles"?

SCENE SEVENTY-SIX
THE WOMAN WITH THE PERFUME[135]

When Jesus had finished talking, a man wearing a long black robe and the smell of incense was the first to approach him.

"That's Simon," Jesna whispered. "He's a Pharisee."

"Jesna."

"Yes, Priscilla."

"It seems like wherever we go one or two men wearing black robes are there. I know they are Pharisees, but I thought Pharisees were scribes in the Temple in Jerusalem. What are they doing out in the countryside, this far from Jerusalem?"

"You're very observant, Priscilla. If a Pharisee is this far from his home base, it's very likely he is on a spying mission. He's been sent out from the rulers of the temple."

"But why would anyone want to spy on Jesus? He's just traveling around talking about God's love, healing people?"

"But look around, Priscilla. He also attracts a large following wherever he goes. Anyone with this kind of influence will make people in authority nervous. They fear he might turn the masses against them. The 'spies' are sent to sniff out any potential problems."

Simon asked Jesus if he would be willing to come to his house that evening for dinner. Jesus agreed, even though Pete was screaming, "Don't go! It's a trap!" in his ear.

We followed Jesus back into a small village. So did half of the crowd. He stopped in front of the synagogue and sat down on the stone patio of the courtyard. For a couple of hours, while waiting for dinner, he talked and listened to the people.

A woman wearing a bright purple dress seemed very interested in what Jesus was saying, especially when he talked about being made "clean and new." She asked no questions, but caught every word as it left his mouth. Her eyes were open windows to a troubled soul.

Eventually one of Jesus' disciples tapped him on the arm and said that it was time to go to Simon's house. Jesus stood up, dusted himself off, and walked on down the street. The woman in purple hurriedly walked in the opposite direction. The rest of the crowd disappeared into the warm night air.

Entering Simon's house, Jesus was instructed by a servant to take a place at the dinner table. His disciples were led into another room. Just as Jesus was being served, the woman in purple came through Simon's front door and race-walked over to where Jesus sat. She was clutching a stone bottle that filled the room with the scent of a thousand flowers—even with the top still in place.

She stopped at Jesus' feet. Her eyes were fountains that sent thin streams of tears over her cheekbones and splashing down on his dusty feet. As the guests squirmed uncomfortably, she reached back and pulled the veil off her hair. This loosed a brown cascade that fell over her shoulders and down to her waist. She bent over and continued washing Jesus' feet with her tears. Her long hair became a towel that dried them clean.

Simon and his other guests continued to act as if their robes were infested with ants. They looked on in horror and began to murmur their displeasure. But they hadn't seen everything yet.

When Jesus' feet were clean, the woman took the stone top from the perfume jar and poured the entire, sweet-smelling contents onto his feet. The crowd gasped, and then erupted with commentary.

"That's the most expensive perfume you can buy!"

"It's a year's wages down the drain."

"Get her out of here!"

"That money could've been given to the synagogue!"

"Simon, make that harlot leave. She's defiling your house."

"I knew that man was not a prophet. If he were he would have known the woman is a sinner."

Jesus slowly rose and stood on his freshly washed feet. When he reached his full height, he reached out and helped the woman in purple to her feet as well.

"Simon, I have something to say to you."

"Oh? Tell me then."

"Two men were in debt. One owed five hundred pieces of silver; the other owed fifty. Neither of the two could pay. The man they owed was kind, however. Instead of sending them to jail—as was his right—he forgave both debts. Which of the two would be more grateful?"

"That's easy. The one who was forgiven most."

"That's right.

"This woman has been forgiven much, but you only a little.

"I came to your house, Simon, and you did not offer me water to wash my feet—although that is the custom. You did not greet me at the door—although that is the custom. You provided me nothing for freshening up from the day—although that is the custom.

"But this woman rained tears on my feet and dried them with

her hair. She kissed my feet and soothed them with fine perfume. It is not the custom for a 'harlot,' as you say, to act with such social grace. And it's also not the custom for anyone to say this: 'Daughter, I forgive your sins. You are washed clean. Your heart is perfume to God, your Father. Go and live in peace.'"

The woman hugged Jesus with all her might and went running from Simon's home. Her cries of joy echoed in the night.

Simon's house echoed with angry words. "Who does he think he is, forgiving sins?"

Jesus turned and walked out of Simon's house. His disciples followed. He had not eaten, but he appeared to have had a stomach full of the Pharisee's self-righteous pie.

FAMILY DISCUSSION

1. How would you describe the woman's feelings as she ran through the streets?

2. What do you think made her so happy?

SCENE SEVENTY-SEVEN
THE MINISTERING WOMEN[136]

After leaving Simon's house, Jesus and his friends went outside the village and set up camp. They gathered wood, built a fire, and unrolled their blankets. But there was something missing. Pete was the first to notice.

"Are they going to sleep without having anything to eat?" he asked.

"They don't have any food, Pete. They ate the last of their food for breakfast this morning."

"Well, can't Jesus send someone out for a giant pizza or a five-gallon bucket of chicken?"

"They don't have any money, either."

"I've got a few bucks. They can have that."

"It's a quite a few centuries before anyone will know what a 'buck' is, Pete. But that's very nice of you to offer."

"Yeah, little brother, what's gotten into you lately? You're only obnoxious about half the time now."

No one in camp complained about an empty stomach and no one asked Jesus to do anything, although more than one belly grumbled as the disciples were preparing to sleep. But before the first disciple could make the trip to dreamland, the sounds of snapping twigs and grinding gravel were heard. Someone was approaching.

Jesus and the disciples peered into the night to see the uninvited guest. My nose already knew.

Within seconds the source of the noise had stepped into the light of the camp fire—it was six sandaled feet, attached to three brightly robed women.

"Mary," Jesus said, "how are you?"

"That can't be Jesus' mother," Pete blurted out. "She's too young."

"No, Pete. The woman Jesus is talking to, the one with the yellow scarf over her head, is Mary Magdalene."

"Oh," Pete said, "I remember her. She's the woman that Jesus made seven demons move out of."

"That's right, Pete. That's Mary Magdalene. The one to her right is Joanna, wife of Chuza, Herod's manager. The other lady is Susanna."

"Old Susanna?" Pete asked with a grin.

"No, Pete, not 'O, Susanna,'" Jesna said while rolling her eyes.

Each woman was carrying a big straw basket. The smell of fresh bread and roasted meat was overpowering. It was enough to make a time-warped dog salivate.

Mary Magdalene was the first to speak. "We heard that Simon probably isn't going to be joining up with you anytime soon." Jesus smiled. "And we thought you might be able to use some food."

The three women then set about spreading a picnic feast on the ground by the fire. They also left a small pouch that jingled with the sound of coins. The disciples gathered around. They seemed as excited as kids at a birthday party.

Jesus looked on, still smiling. As the last dish was set, he looked up into the night sky and whispered, "Once more, Father, you have sent ravens to feed your prophets. Glory to your name. And blessings on your servants here."

Their job done, the three friends fluttered off into the night.

FAMILY DISCUSSION

1. When was the last time that God did an unexpected favor for you?

2. What did it feel like, to be remembered by God?

SCENE SEVENTY-EIGHT
YOU CAN'T GET ALONG WITH THE DEVIL[137]

Jesus and his disciples continued on foot from town to town and crisscrossed the Sea of Galilee by boat. Many nights they slept under sky instead of a roof. And on many of those nights they were soaked by rain and shivered dry in the wind.

But Jesus continued undaunted, spreading the word about his Father's love and his Father's kingdom. He continued on as summer sizzled, as fall fell and blew away, as winter seized and withdrew, and finally, as spring came visiting again. All of this time he and his disciples lived on the mercy gifts of the crowds who came out to listen.

One day, not far from his home town of Nazareth, Jesus finished speaking and was immediately approached by a man who pulled on his sleeve with one hand and pointed at his own mouth with the other.

Jesus touched the man on the lips and delivered him from a demon that had kept him mute for a long time. The man instantly became a motormouth. His newfound tongue was like a child's favorite Christmas present.

"Would you listen to that?" Pete said. "He's going to get arrested for talking past the speed limit. Way past the speed limit! I can hardly hear that fast!"

As the man blabbered joyfully, the crowd began to murmur. Before long, the murmuring heated to a rolling boil, fired by a band of black-robed agitators. Pete was right. Someone was about to get scalded with trouble. But it wasn't the fast talker.

"Black Magic!" shouted a bearded man in black.

"Look who's talking about *black* magic," Pete said, and I scooted out of the way just as he poked Priscilla.

"He's doing these tricks by the power of Satan!" another howled.

The poor man who had been set free, suddenly shut up. He put his fingers to his lips and pressed them closed. He appeared confused, perhaps not knowing if his words—his new toys—were gifts from God or from the Devil.

Jesus walked over and put his arm around the healed man's shoulder. "Don't be afraid," he whispered. Then he turned and faced his accusers:

"Any country in civil war for very long is wasted. A constantly squabbling family falls to pieces."

The Pilgrims stood to attention and became mute themselves.

"If Satan cancels Satan, is there any Satan left? You accuse me of ganging up with the Devil, the prince of demons, to cast out demons, but if you're slinging devil mud at me, calling me a devil who kicks out devils, doesn't the same mud stick to your own exorcists? But if it's *God's* finger I'm pointing that sends the demons on their way, then God's kingdom is here for sure."[138]

The bubbling crowd simmered down. Jesus had once again turned an offensive move of the Pharisees into his checkmate.

"Thank you," the former mute said to Jesus. Then he turned and talked his way home.

Most of the crowd began to nod their agreement to the logic of Jesus. The men in black said nothing. But their faces became bright red.

"Jesna," Priscilla said.

"Yes."

"What exactly, or who exactly, is 'Satan?' I mean, I've seen a few horror movies, but I don't really know who he is."

Jesna took a deep breath and quickly scanned the sky for the best answer.

"Satan is, er, was, an angelic creation of God. He was originally a beautiful being of light. But something very terrible happened."

"What, Jesna."

"God has given each of his creatures freedom. He's not Geppetto—he didn't make any puppets. There are no strings attached to his creations. Everything he crafted has the ability to choose life with him in the kingdom, or life away from him in darkness.

"Satan did something beastly. He began to listen more to his own pride and selfish ambition than to the voice of God. He decided he wanted to be equal with, or even above, his Creator. When he set his mind for this, he tripped over his aspirations and fell from God's kingdom. He set up his own.

"Satan rules a kingdom that is, in every way, the opposite to the kingdom of God. Love, peace, joy, and freedom are the very air in God's kingdom. Satan's subjects breathe fear, anger, despair, and bondage.

"At the heart of Jesus' ministry here on earth is life, life in full, for all those who are living in the domain of Satan, and those who have not decided where to live."

"But Jesna, how do people know which kingdom they are living in or if they are in some in-between place?"

"If in your heart you want to live in God's kingdom of love, just tell him. He'll make all the travel arrangements. If your life is already ripe with the fruit of his kingdom—love, peace, and joy—you're already there."

"Jesna."

"Yes, Priscilla."

"I want to live in God's kingdom."

Jesna was beaming like a child on Christmas morning. "Then tell him," She said while pointing to Jesus.

Priscilla nodded her desire to Jesus.

He beamed a broad smile back to her and gave her a "thumbs up" sign. It was his second big catch of the day.

FAMILY DISCUSSION

1. Think of any ways your own family is divided. Do you squabble persistently? Confess your own part in the family battles and resolve to dance to the beat of a different King.

2. Anyone can join God's kingdom by just asking to be a part. Have you asked yet? Tell about it.

SCENE SEVENTY-NINE
THE SIN AGAINST
THE HOLY SPIRIT[139]

"Hey, Jesus!" One of the Pharisees shouted—and from the tone of his voice it sounded like he might be about to challenge Jesus
to another chess match.

"Suppose I say you are right," he sneered. "Suppose you are"
(and he pointed up to the sky) "his messenger. Then aren't all of
us who questioned your authority—saying that it comes from
Satan—guilty of blasphemy? Are our souls lost forever, now?"

Jesus smiled. "I'm glad you are thinking about the condition
of your soul."

The Pharisee's sneer doubled in volume.

Jesus continued:

"There's nothing done or said that can't be forgiven. But if
you deliberately persist in your slanders against God's Spirit,
you are repudiating the very One who forgives. If you reject
the Son of Man out of some misunderstanding, the Holy Spirit
can forgive you, but when you reject the Holy Spirit, you're
sawing off the branch on which you're sitting, severing by your
own perversity all connections with the One who forgives.

"If you grow a healthy tree, you'll pick healthy fruit. If you
grow a diseased tree, you'll pick worm-eaten fruit. The fruit
tells you about the tree."[140]

"You, Jesus. You are the blasphemer!" The angry Pharisee was
pointing at Jesus with a trembling finger. "Did you all hear what
he just said? How dare you set rules on blasphemy! May," (and he

again looked at the sky instead of saying "God") "never forgive you!"

Pete snorted, "Whew! What is this all about?"

"You need to understand, Pete, that the Jews—especially the Pharisees—do a meticulous job of keeping the third commandment, 'Thou shalt not take the name of Jehovah thy God in vain.' You noticed he wouldn't even speak God's name. When they need to write his name they leave the vowels out so no one will accidentally pronounce it and blaspheme.

"Jesus was saying, in essence, 'You go too far with some things, and not far enough with others. God can forgive what comes out of your mouth. But what is truly important is what is in your heart. If it is connected to God, through His Holy Spirit, it will be filled with love and life and you'll bear good fruit. If this connection is severed, you're in severe trouble. If you don't value the connection and the Holy Spirit—which is the life blood that flows through it—you're doomed.'"

"Jesna."

"Yes, Mr. Pilgrim."

"You'll never believe how many times I've heard people question if they've accidentally, you know, committed the unpardonable sin of blaspheming the Holy Spirit. But you're saying that might not be such an easy thing to do?"

"Exactly. That's what Jesus was saying to the man in black—that you can be meticulous to avoid 'blasphemy' while having no Holy Spirit life in your limbs, no fruit in your branches."

"So," Pete interrupted, "it doesn't matter if someone has carved a bad word on your trunk; but you better keep your roots in the ground if you want to stay alive. And some people in this crowd have clean-as-a-whistle trunks that are as dead as the Petrified Forest."

"Pete."

"Yes, Jesna."

"I think you're about ready to be a tour guide."

FAMILY DISCUSSION

1. How did the Jews honor the name of God?

2. How would you expect someone to act if he is rooted in the Holy Spirit?

3. How does one become rooted in the Holy Spirit?

SCENE EIGHTY
THE SIGN OF JONAH[141]

The Pharisee who had rebuked Jesus was still pointing at him in trembling rage. The purple veins in his forehead were throbbing. Several of his friends approached him and talked to him in low tones. Their words seemed to calm him. It wasn't long until he had put his finger back in its holster. One of his comforters picked up his part in the conversation.

"Jesus, perhaps my friend here was a bit harsh on you. You have made some, well, pretty extraordinary claims." The man was speaking in smooth, almost condescending tones.

"Maybe you would do us—and this crowd—a favor and show us your divine credentials. You know, do a miracle or something to prove that you are worthy to speak for God."

"Is that man a used-camel salesman or something? I like candy, but all that sugar coating is about to make me hurl," and Pete acted as if he were about to be sick.

It must've gotten to Jesus too. He hurled out some pretty strong words:

"You're looking for proof, but you're looking for the wrong kind. All you want is something to titillate your curiosity, satisfy your lust for miracles. The only proof you're going to get is what looks like the absence of proof: Jonah-evidence. Like Jonah, three days and nights in the fish's belly, the Son of Man will be gone three days and nights in a deep grave."[142]

"Pssst, Jesna, I need a little help here. What did that mean? It sounds *real* important. But it went *whisssp,* right over my head."

"Well, it was sort of a double-entendre, Priscilla."

"Double the tundra. What? Now you are over *my* head," Pete said.

"Sorry, Pete. It means a double meaning.

"Jesus is comparing the group of Pharisees to the people in the wicked city of Nineveh, you know the place where God sent Jonah to preach."

"Yeah, I remember. I'm not a total Bible-ignoramus. Jonah was too afraid to go, so he ran away. But God sent a big-ole fish to gobble him up and then puke him up, right into a pulpit. Correct?"

"Pretty close, Pete. But Jesus was just making the comparison of his accusers to the godless folks of Nineveh. And that's pretty hard for a self-righteous Pharisee to stomach.

"Then he said that the only miracle they would see would be one like the Ninevites saw. Jesus is looking ahead to his death. He's saying that he will be buried in the earth for the same amount of time that Jonah was in the whale. But the tomb won't be able to hold him. He will come out of it. This will be the sign they will get—the proof that he is who he claims to be. It's the ultimate proof. Even death will not be able to hold him. When that happens they will know the authority with which he speaks. And if they're wise, they'll respond the same way the Ninevites did—with ears and hearts thrown wide open."

FAMILY DISCUSSION

1. What are some ways you know God through having "proofs"?

2. What are some other ways you know him without any "proofs"?

SCENE EIGHTY-ONE
THE RETURN OF AN EVIL SPIRIT[143]

Jesus continued his speech to the small group of Pharisees. The crowd sat glued to the debate as if they were watching the last few seconds of a championship game. "You would all be wise to listen to what I am about to say:

"When a defiling evil spirit is expelled from someone, it drifts along through the desert looking for an oasis, some unsuspecting soul it can bedevil. When it doesn't find anyone, it says, 'I'll go back to my old haunt.' On return it finds the person spotlessly clean, but vacant."

"The Holy Spirit has not been invited to move in," inserted Jesna.

"It then runs out and rounds up seven other spirits more evil than itself and they all move in, whooping it up. That person ends up far worse off than if he'd never gotten cleaned up in the first place."[144]

Each of the Pharisees' purpled foreheads were awash with perspiration.

"Do you see?" shouted the former finger wagger. "And did you hear? I think he was talking about us, the true keepers of the law."

"No way," said another. "He may be misguided but he's not insane."

"Was he talking about them, Jesna? Have they got some uninvited house guests they don't know anything about?"

"Listen, Pete. He'll tell them."

Jesus looked like pictures of Superman I had seen on the Pilgrims' TV. The Pharisees' eyes were shooting laser beams of anger that were bouncing off Jesus with no effect. He did not beam anger back at them. He just absorbed what they sent and returned a warm, sad smile.

"What I have said describes this generation," he said, "especially those who attempt righteousness through their own efforts. You may have put your houses in order—made them clean—but I have preached the kingdom message to you. I have told you that God is willing and ready to move into your 'houses,' your 'temples,' but you have not invited him in.

"So now beware: devils of pride, self-righteousness, arrogance, strife, complacency, judgment, and anger are moving back in. Send them away; invite me in. I'll put your houses in order."

FAMILY DISCUSSION

1. What do you think the Pharisees are feeling as Jesus is telling them their "good behavior" is not what God is looking for?

2. What does it mean to you that God wants more from you than good behavior?

SCENE EIGHTY-TWO
JESUS' TRUE FAMILY[145]

The pack of Pharisees had apparently heard all they could stand without their heads exploding. They spun around as one and marched off through the middle of the crowd. A low-lying cloud of dust followed at their heels.

A handful of people fell in line in the dust behind the departing Pharisees. The majority of listeners, however, closed ranks and continued acting like a nest full of hungry baby birds, eagerly awaiting another meal of words from Jesus.

Jesus began teaching again. But he had not taught long before a man was tugging on his sleeve for a private word.

Jesna inched the car closer so we could hear.

"Jesus, your mother and brothers are in the crowd. They've been trying to get a message to you, to let you know they are here."

Jesus smiled but didn't respond directly. All four Pilgrims began craning their necks, trying to pick out familiar faces from the crowd.

"I bet I find her first," Pete said, once he realized the whole family was on a visual treasure hunt for Mary's kind face.

While they were scanning the crowd it hit Pete what the man had just told Jesus. "Wait a minute! I didn't know Jesus had brothers. Did they have God for a father, too?"

"No, Pete, they're Jesus' younger brothers, the natural-born sons of Mary and Joseph."

"Can you imagine having Jesus as an older brother?" Pete said. "I mean it's bad enough having Priscilla for an older monster, I mean, sister. But, I bet they'd always be hearing, '*Jesus* always eats his broccoli,' and 'Why can't you be as smart as your older brother?'"

"I think Mary and Joseph would have been a bit more sensitive than that, Pete," Jesna said. "Now, let's listen."

"Who do you think my mother and brothers are?" Jesus was asking the man who had tugged on his sleeve.

Jesus then stretched out his hand toward his disciples, and as he made a broad sweeping motion he said, "Look closely. These are my mother and brothers. And so are you."

"Obedience is thicker than blood. The person who obeys my heavenly Father's will is my brother and sister and mother."[146]

"Is Jesus disowning his family?" Priscilla asked.

"No, Priscilla! Not only will he never disown them, it would be impossible for anyone to love his earthly family more than he does.

"But he's here on a special mission. He's establishing a kingdom outpost on the Devil's turf, and he couldn't resist the opportunity to teach his disciples something very important. He wants them to realize how strong the bonds of love are for people in the kingdom.

"He's told them how to get in—through willing obedience to the rules of the King. Now he wants them to know that in the kingdom everyone is family. They are bound tightly together by bonds of family love.

"The love-ties he has to the disciples—the same ones they should have to each other—are even stronger and more binding than those of family love.

"If you really love others, then it's easy to keep the 'golden rule': it's easy to love your neighbor (your sister, brother, parents, children) as much as you love yourself. You're all family."

"You know," Pete said, "I don't know about love in the 'kingdom,' but I think I understand how strong family-love is because one time Dad told me he would give up his own life for his family. He said he was willing to die for us. Now that's some kind of special love, isn't it?"

Mr. Pilgrim was blushing.

"Yes it is, Pete. Being willing to lay down your life for your family is the strongest love in the universe. And it's the kind of love Jesus has for Mary, his brothers, his disciples, and for each of you. That's kingdom-family love."

FAMILY DISCUSSION

1. How does it feel to know that you are as much a part of Jesus' family as his mother and brothers?

2. What does the Bible mean when it says "Obedience is thicker than blood?"

SCENE EIGHTY-THREE
THE PARABLE OF THE SOWER[147]

In the early afternoon, while shadows were still smaller than life, Jesus was bringing his daily teachings to a close. After his last story he called his mother and brothers to come to him. Mary beamed a proud smile as she made the distance between them disappear. It had been more than a year since Jesus had seen his mother. The last time was on the day when his hometown "friends" had tried to throw him over a cliff.

"Mary is in her mid-forties now," Jesna said quietly. She still had the same youthful smile and sparkling eyes we had seen the day Gabriel told her she was to be the mother of Jesus. But her hair was dusted with white now; and her face, though still beautiful, had been weathered by the Nazarene sun.

Jesus gave his mother a long hug and introduced her and his brothers to the crowd. Many applauded. One shouted, "It's the mother of the Messiah."

The crowd respected Jesus' desire to spend some time with his family. No one approached him for a miracle. For the next couple of hours Jesus was brought up-to-date concerning the village of Nazareth.

Once Mr. Pilgrim commented, "This is incredible! We're getting to hear a conversation between the Son of God and his earthly mother—two people that will have a zillion statues and paintings made of them—and they haven't said the first word about theology; they're talking about who's married, who's had children, and the carpentry business. It's like they're just plain folks."

"Maybe they know that it is far more important for theology to be lived by 'just plain folks' than to be discussed and debated by scholars, Mr. Pilgrim," Jesna offered.

A thoughtful smile broke across Mr. Pilgrim's face. "I like that," he said. "That means even I could be a theologian."

"You already are," Jesna said.

When Jesus realized that Mary and his brothers barely had enough time to get back home before dark, he brought their conversation to a close.

They all hugged goodbye and Jesus explained that it would be a while longer before he would come to Nazareth. Mary nodded her understanding, and then told the Creator of the universe to be careful and to get plenty of sleep. His brothers waved goodbye until they disappeared in the evening dusk.

Jesus and his disciples traveled northeast toward the Sea of Galilee. It took them the final two hours of daylight and half of the next day to make it.

We drove along behind. The trip was mostly downhill, and rarely flat. The last quarter-mile took us through a wheat field that grew in hundreds of patches (some small, some large) on both sides of the rocky path we traveled over.

We stopped and set up camp when our road ran into the Sea of Galilee.

"Boy," Pete said, "it seems like for Jesus, all roads lead to this big lake, huh?"

"I'm glad he likes it so much," Mrs. Pilgrim said. "It's the most beautiful area I've seen anywhere. I wouldn't mind having a lake-front house right here."

"But we'd all be crushed to death, Mom," Pete quipped.

Everyone looked puzzled.

"I mean if you got it right now, it would be on top of us because we're not solid."

There were still more puzzled looks than smiles.

Late that afternoon Jesus was back at it—teaching by the sea.

In a couple of days the crowd of listeners had grown so large that Jesus had to get into a boat and drift out into the lake. The boat became his pulpit and the lake water a microphone. With a multitude crowded to the water's edge, he taught them using many stories.

One of them went like this:

"Listen. What do you make of this? A
farmer planted seed. As he scattered the
seed, some of it fell on the road and
birds ate it."

"He needed a good scarecrow, didn't
he Dad?"
"Shhh, Pete."

"Some fell in the gravel; it
sprouted quickly but didn't put
down roots, so when the sun came
up it withered just as quickly. Some fell in the weeds; as it came
up, it was strangled among the weeds and nothing came of it.
Some fell on good earth and came up with a flourish, produc-
ing a harvest exceeding his wildest dreams."[148]

The crowd was silent and frozen to Jesus' every word. So it
was very surprising when he added: "Are you listening to this story? Really listening? If you have 'ears,' let it change your life."

FAMILY DISCUSSION

1. If a person were "really listening" to Jesus' story about seed
   and soils, what would he have heard?

2. What kind of ears does Jesus want you to have?

SCENE EIGHTY-FOUR
THE REASON FOR SPEAKING IN PARABLES[149]

Later that evening we were sitting beside Jesus and his disciples around a crackling campfire. They had finished eating a meal of roasted fish and bread and were having a lazy conversation before turning in for the night.

One of the disciples asked Jesus a question that must have been on the minds of all the others, judging from the way they all nodded their heads after it was asked.

"Jesus, why do you tell the people so many stories? Wouldn't it be easier for them to understand if you told them straight out what you mean?"

"That's a very good question," Priscilla said. "I've been wanting to ask him that for a long time."

Jesus stared at the fire and poked it with a long stick before answering. After at least a minute had passed in silence, he looked at the disciple who had asked the question. The fire reflected in both sets of eyes.

"I speak in parables, in stories, to create a readiness in the hearts of those listening. You see, people of this world are often held captive by the 'Thief and Robber,' the 'Prince of the World.' My stories are like music. They slip past the guard that holds their hearts captive and lonely prisoners. Their hearts hear my songs and long to be free—to go home. The guard does not realize what is happening. He does not realize that communication to the soul has slipped past his watch.

"You are all blessed, and have been given insight into God's kingdom. You know how it works. The door is open for you and your heart comes freely to me. Others need help to be set free.

My stories are the music I sing for them, music that can slip under their cell doors and open their blind eyes. Music that can set them free from their chains and lead them home.

"If I spoke more directly the message would not get through. It would be intercepted by the guard or by their own reasoning mind. The soul would remain in prison. It would have eyes but see nothing, open ears that understand nothing. That's why I speak in parables."

"Wow!" Pete said. "And I thought it was because people don't go to sleep so fast when you tell a story."

"That, too, Pete," Jesus said with a wink.

FAMILY DISCUSSION

1. Tell the others which Bible story is your favorite. Tell why you like it so much.

2. What did Jesus mean when he was talking about the message he was trying to get across being intercepted by their own minds?

SCENE EIGHTY-FIVE
WHAT THE PARABLE OF THE SOWER MEANS[150]

"Jesus," another of the disciples said sheepishly, "what if someone doesn't get the meaning of one of your stories?"

"Got anyone in mind, Judas?" a disciple asked before Jesus had time to answer.

Jesus held back his words and looked at Judas.

"Well, I'm not so sure I got that last story you told today—about the scattered seeds."

"My stories don't always have the same exact meaning for everyone, Judas. It's sort of like it is with songs. The singer is more interested in whether or not it makes his listeners want to dance more than if it makes them want to dissect the meaning of the lyrics. Do my stories make you want to dance, Judas?"

Judas quickly looked at the ground. He said nothing.

Jesus broke the silence between them. "That story does have a meaning. It's this:

"When anyone hears news of the kingdom and doesn't take it in, it just remains on the surface, and so the Evil One comes along and plucks it right out of the person's heart. This is the seed the farmer scatters on the road.

"The seed cast in the gravel—this is the person who hears and instantly responds with enthusiasm. But there is no soil of character, and so when the emotions wear off and some difficulty arrives, there is nothing to show for it.

"The seed cast in the weeds is the person who hears the kingdom news, but weeds of worry and illusions about getting more and wanting everything under the sun strangle what is heard, and nothing comes of it."

Jesus gave Judas a compassionate gaze. His eyes were wet.

"The seed cast on good earth is the person who hears and takes in the News, and then produces a harvest beyond his wildest dreams."[151]

"Pssst."

"Yes, Pete," Jesna said softly.

"So the 'seeds' are Jesus' stories about the kingdom?"

"That's right."

"And the dirt is what type of person you are?"

"Yes, Pete. What type of person you are, how attached to this world you are, and how ready you are to accept kingdom-love into your heart."

"But, Jesna, what's this business about a 'harvest?' What kind of plants can grow out of a person's chest?"

"That's a wonderful question, Pete. Kingdom-seeds planted in fertile soul-soil grow delicious fruit."

"Huh?"

"The fruits of the kingdom in a person's life, the primary ones, are love, peace, and joy."

The snapping of a twig called our attention back to the conversation Jesus was having with Judas. Judas stood to his feet and turned to walk away from the campfire.

"What's wrong with Judas?" Pete asked.

Jesna stared at her lap. "I guess you could say he heard the song, but doesn't want to dance."

A tear was sliding down Jesus' face. Not only was he losing a dance partner but a whole lap full of kingdom seeds had just spilled to the rocky ground.

FAMILY DISCUSSION

1. Do you remember the first time that kingdom-seeds were planted in your heart?

2. What kinds of fruit have been growing since that time?

SCENE EIGHTY-SIX
"HE WHO HAS EARS TO HEAR, LET HIM HEAR"[152]

As Judas walked away, deeper into the darkness, Jesus continued talking to the other eleven:

"Take heed what you hear; the measure you give to others will be the measure you get, and still more will be given to you. For if you have, more will be given...."

He glanced to where Judas had been swallowed up by the night before continuing:

"And from him who has not, even what he has will be taken away."[153]

The other disciples were staring soberly at the fire. The light flickering across their faces made it seem they were acting in an old silent movie. Maybe that's why no one spoke out the obvious question.

Pete could not stand their silence. "Well, that's just not fair! Why should the ones who have a lot get more? And why do the ones that don't have much get that taken from them?"

"When did you become a communist, little brother?"

Jesna stepped between them. "Pete's question is very fair, Priscilla. And the answer has nothing to do with communism, or even Robin Hood, for that matter.

"A seed that is growing into a plant in good soil will begin to put out bigger and bigger shoots and roots. And as it grows it will naturally take in more nutrients from the soil, more water and sunlight. The larger it becomes, the more it receives from the environment. Right?"

"Yeah," Pete answered. "And the plant growing in the gravel will start to die."

"Yes. And as it dies it will begin to take in less and less.

"It's the same with kingdom-seeds growing in a person's heart. The bigger they grow, the more nutrients are taken in and the more fruits (love, peace, and joy) are given out. Plus, when someone gives kingdom-seeds away to others, the receivers usually become givers—returning as much or more than they received."

Priscilla was punching on her wrist computer. "I believe it would be fair to call what Jesus is saying the 'Law of Reciprocal Dividends.'"

"The law of re-sipping what?" Pete asked with a corkscrew face.

"Your sister said, Pete, that in the kingdom, no matter how much love you pour out for others, God will give you even more to take its place.

"You can't be selfish with God's love. They more you take in for yourself, the more you will give out to others. But" (and she too glanced at the hole Judas had made in the night), "if the soil of your character is rocky and hard, God's love won't take root, and your kingdom-fruit will die on the vine."

FAMILY DISCUSSION

1. If someone were picking kingdom-fruit from your life, what type of fruit would have the biggest harvest?

2. Are there other kingdom fruits you should grow? Would you share one or two?

SCENE EIGHTY-SEVEN
SEEDS GROWING SECRETLY[154]

Jesus continued teaching the eleven by the blaze of the campfire. He often raised his head and looked out into the darkness as he spoke; perhaps hoping Judas was listening from the edge of the blackness of his self-exile.

"God's kingdom is like seed thrown on a field by a man who then goes to bed and forgets about it. The seed sprouts and grows—he has no idea how it happens. The earth does it all without his help: first a green stem of grass, then a bud, then the ripened grain. When the grain if fully formed—harvest time!"[155]

"You know," Priscilla said, "It's amazing how much people, even scientists" (she said that word almost reverently) "don't know."

"What do you mean, Prissy? I thought you Spockettes knew everything."

"Nope. I don't know any more about how seeds grow than the man in Jesus' story. I don't know how a corn seed knows how to collect just the right chemicals from the ground to make a giant corn stalk, instead of a leafy vine with watermelons growing from it."

"You don't?"

"No, I don't know how that happens. Even scientists who write biology textbooks claiming that people evolved from other forms of life, don't know how the very *first* cell got here—and one living cell is more complicated than, well, than my wrist computer."

"So what's your point? You're making me kinda scared thinking that people I thought were smart, ain't."

"Aren't, Pete. Aren't," Mrs. Pilgrim corrected. Pete ignored her.

"I have two points, Pete," Priscilla said.

"I thought you'd have two points. One wouldn't be enough of a challenge for you. So let's hear 'em."

"First, if God knows so much more about the mystery of plant life than the scientists who have been studying the subject at universities all around the world, he probably knows at least that much more about spiritual life—kingdom-seeds. Human scientists have hardly cracked the covers of those books."

"And?" Pete coaxed.

"And it would seem the smart thing to do would be to invite God to plant a secret garden in our hearts and then trust the growing seed to him."

Pete was pursing his lips and thoughtfully nodding his head.

"Priscilla, that's a very wise and humble thing for a young scientist to say," said Jesna.

I had to bark in agreement.

FAMILY DISCUSSION

1. Have you allowed God to plant a secret garden in your heart? What does it look like to others when all the flowers are in bloom?

2. What kind of kingdom-plant do you want to be?

SCENE EIGHTY-EIGHT
THE PARABLE OF THE TARES[156]

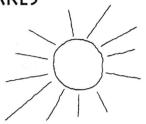

The night passed. Morning found Judas back in the fold, sleeping next to a circle of embers, within the larger circle of disciples. The early morning rays of sunlight were filtering through our olive tree canopy. The light served as a morning wake-up call for Jesus and the disciples—who began sitting up and stretching in thirteen different directions.

But when they made it to their feet and began to stir around preparing breakfast, Pete suggested that we walk back to the shore where Jesus had been preaching the day before. Pete probably wanted to put a little distance between his stomach and the alluring smells of bread, dates, and cheese.

We walked away from the olive tree bed and breakfast toward the glistening, blue face of the Sea of Galilee. Along the way we again passed in and out of patchy growths of wheat. Pete couldn't resist turning his arms into airplane wings and gliding through the golden clouds of bread seeds. It wasn't long until he was acting out a dramatic spinning, tumbling crash into a three point landing. From his sitting position he broke off a stalk.

"That's a tare," Jesna said.

Pete stopped short and inspected his pants. "What do you mean? I have a tear? I don't see no tear."

"No, not a pants tear. A plant tare."

"Huh?"

"A tare is a plant—a type of rye grass—that often grows mixed in with the wheat."

"So? What's so bad about eating rye grass? Cows eat grass; and Dad eats rye bread sandwiches."

"That's very different, Pete. Tares, like the one in your hand with the reddish growth on it, often have fungus growing on them."

Pete tossed the broken stalk away and stood up, brushing his pants. "That's disgusting! What kind of fungus?"

"In tares it's a serious poison if eaten by humans. It could kill you."

Pete rocketed his way out of the wheat and tares.

"Why don't the farmers pull those tares out?" Mr. Pilgrim asked. "I mean, since they could kill somebody, my goodness!"

"Because—especially when the wheat and tares are young—it's almost impossible to tell them apart. They look the same. It's only about now, when both kinds of plant mature and form heads, that you can see the difference."

"Well, it's a pretty big difference—bread for life or bread for death by poison."

"That's right, Mr. Pilgrim. There is a huge difference between wheat and tares. I believe you'll hear Jesus talking about that later today."

And she was right.

By midmorning Jesus had joined us by the sea, and a crowd had once again gathered around him. He had been talking about the differences between God's kingdom and the Devil's kingdom when he told a story that got Pete's attention:

"God's kingdom is like a farmer who planted good seed in his field. That night, while his hired men were asleep, his enemy sowed thistles (tares) all through the wheat and slipped away before dawn. When the first green shoots appeared and the grain began to form, the thistles showed up, too.

"The farmhands came to the farmer and said, 'Master, that was clean seed you planted, wasn't it? Where did these thistles come from?'

"He answered, 'Some enemy did this.'

"The farmhands asked, 'Should we weed out the thistles?'

"He said, 'No, if you weed the thistles, you'll pull up the wheat, too. Let them grow together until harvest time. Then I'll instruct the harvesters to pull up the thistles and tie them in bundles for the fire, then gather the wheat and put it in the barn.'"[157]

The crowd was as silent as a wheat field on a windless day.

Pete was the first to speak. "You know, Dad, it sounds like there's a fungus among us."

"In more ways than one, Pete. In more ways than one."

FAMILY DISCUSSION

1. Describe some ways in which wheat-people act differently from tare-people.

2. How would you explain Jesus' parable about "wheat" and "tares" to someone?

SCENE EIGHTY-NINE
THE PARABLE OF THE MUSTARD SEED[158]

"Can you all see this?" Jesus asked the crowd. He had stood up and was holding something on the tip of the index finger of his right hand.

"I can't see a thing," Pete announced. "Let's get closer."

We all moved toward Jesus for a closer inspection.

"I still can't see way up there. Dad, put me on your shoulders."

Mr. Pilgrim gave Pete a spinning hoist to his shoulders. As Pete sat with his legs dangling down in front of his dad's chest he began to eyeball the tip of Jesus' finger with squinting eyes.

"Whatever it is, it's real small."

"Duh," Priscilla said from her earthbound position. "I didn't think he could balance a watermelon up there."

"This is a mustard seed," Jesus said. "The kingdom of heaven is like this."

"Describe it for us, Pete," Mrs. Pilgrim said. "If the kingdom is like that, I'd like to know what it looks like."

"Well, it sorta looks like a yellow BB."

"A what?" Priscilla asked.

"A BB. It's round, and it's yellow, and it's bigger than a flea and smaller than a tick."

I couldn't help scratching a bit after that description.

"(The kingdom of Heaven) is like a grain of mustard seed, which, when sown upon the ground, is the smallest of all the seeds on earth; yet when it is sown it grows up and becomes the greatest of all shrubs, and puts forth large branches, so that the birds of the air can make nests in its shade."[159]

"Look there," Jesus said, as he pointed across the crowd.

"What's he pointing at?" Pete asked.

"There," Jesna said. "In the middle of that patch of wheat, just to the left of that big rock."

I located the target. A thick-stemmed plant—almost a bush — that grew up from the ground as an inverted triangle. Dark green leaves grew from seven or eight stems that reached up toward the sky. The top of the fanning mustard plant was at least ten feet from the ground.

Given my ancestry, it was hard to resist striking a pointing-pose. It was surrounded by black birds, and some had even made a nest in it.

"I don't get it," Pete announced to no one. "How's Jesus' Daddy's kingdom like ketchup seeds and trees?"

"Because, Pete," Jesna answered, "God's kingdom grows in the soil of a person's life, starting from a tiny seed of pure love. If the soil is good, and the person doesn't uproot it, it will grow to a million times its seed size. It can be a shelter for weary and frail creatures. And it will make a million more kingdom-seeds that can be planted."

"And," Pete said proudly, "it makes it possible for you to stomach baloney, too."

"I guess you're right, Pete," Jesna said with a smile and a twinkle in her eye.

FAMILY DISCUSSION

1. Have you ever seen a seed of love grow into something much bigger? Tell about it.

2. What could you do in the next few minutes to plant one of those seeds in your heart?

SCENE NINETY
THE PARABLE OF THE LEAVEN[160]

Jesus spent the rest of the day telling stories by the sea. When Pete tugged on Jesna's sleeve to ask why Jesus was such a storyteller, she said it was to fulfill the prophecy:

"I will open my mouth and tell stories;
I will bring out into the open
things hidden since the world's first day."[161]

"I wish our pastor would tell more stories," Mrs. Pilgrim said. "Look at Pete and Priscilla. They've hardly missed a word that's come out of Jesus' mouth."

The last story to be told by the sea that afternoon was also about the kingdom of God.

Jesus said:

"To what shall I compare the kingdom of God? It is like leaven which a woman took and hid in three measures of flour, till it was all leavened."[162]

"Hey," Pete said. "I remember him talking about the unlevitated bread before. Remind me what the deal is with that stuff again, Jesna."

"Leaven is yeast, Pete."

"Yeah, and it rhymes with heaven, too."

"OK. Leaven rhymes with heaven. And both, to someone who doesn't know how things really work, can seem kind of small, or insignificant. But when leaven gets into your bread dough, or when heaven gets into your heart, there will be a pretty big transformation. Leaven causes what would have been a flat cracker to turn into a towering loaf of soft, (Pete was salivating) chewy, (I was salivating) bread."

"My uncle," Pete said with most of his mind still focused on bread—his eyes were closed and his tongue was circling his lips, "is from Georgia. He said that he was a cracker. Do you think some 'leaven' would help him."

"Some 'heaven' might!" Mr. Pilgrim blurted out, then seemed embarrassed by his own quick response.

"Yes," Jesna said. "I don't know your uncle, but Jesus is talking about putting small amounts of heaven (the kingdom of Heaven) into your heart and standing back to see the transformation."

"From cracker to loafer?" Pete inserted, having returned from his imaginary banquet.

"From cracker to loaf, Pete."

The sun was about ready to punch its time clock when Jesus finished the last story. A family from the audience approached Jesus and invited him and the disciples to come to their house for supper and to spend the night. Jesus accepted, graciously. We followed along in our time-mobile.

Later that evening, while the meal was being prepared and wonderful smells were drifting outside to where Jesus and the disciples were resting in the courtyard, one of the disciples asked Jesus to explain the story about the wheat and tares.

This is what he said:

"The farmer who sows the pure seed is the Son of Man. The field is the world, the pure seeds are subjects of the kingdom, the thistles are subjects of the Devil."

"They're the ones with fungus on them, aren't they Jesna?"

"...and the enemy who sows them is the Devil. The harvest is the end of the age, the curtain of history. The harvest hands are angels."[163]

"That story sounds pretty serious, Jesna," Priscilla said.

"That story is the most serious that can be told, Priscilla. And everyone's life is the pen and paper with which their ending will be written. Whether you mature into ripe subjects in God's kingdom or are 'weeded out' is the ending for you to write."

"Oh my!" Mrs. Pilgrim said. "I had better pay close attention to all these farming lessons."

All Pilgrim heads were nodding. Well, all except Pete's. Pete had disappeared into the night air.

"Hey, where's Petie?" Mr. Pilgrim asked once his head stopped bobbing.

A quick survey of the courtyard revealed that the only people of Pete's height were wearing robes and giggling in Aramaic.

"Oh, he probably just followed his nose to the kitchen," Priscilla said with a shrug of her shoulders. "That's the most likely calculation, don't you think?"

But just then a disturbing sound was heard. The quiet first-century night air was pierced by a high-pitched twenty-first century hum.

"Oh, no!" Jesna said. "That sounds like our car. You don't suppose..."

But we Pilgrims knew Pete. We didn't have to take the time to suppose. Pete had just started the time-mobile and was revving the engine for a solo flight.

Instantly my muscles became steel springs and I was bouncing across the courtyard for the street. Mr. and Mrs. Pilgrim were racing at my tail—helping to set a new world record in the 100-meter sprint and shout.

"Pete!" shouted Mr. Pilgrim.

"Don't touch any buttons!" shouted Mrs. Pilgrim.

"Can I have Pete's room?" shouted Priscilla.

I looked back over my shoulder to see where Jesna was. What I saw was frightening. For the first time in over thirty-two Bible-years Jesna was wearing a look of fear. She was running as fast as her little cherub legs could carry her.

We all dashed out of the courtyard and began to close in on Pete—the would-be astronaut. He was standing up behind the wheel of the time-craft and beaming from ear to ear like a Cheshire cat.

"Hey!" he shouted. "I got it started all by myself. Pretty cool, huh?"

"No, Pete!" Mr. Pilgrim shouted, panting.

"Don't touch anything else!" Mrs. Pilgrim commanded.

"Don't worry," said Pete, "I'm not going to touch anything. But if I were it would be these two flashing red buttons right here."

"No!" shouted Jesna. "Never touch the two red buttons."

But it was too late. Pete's fingers were descending for trouble as he spoke. "What's the big deal about punching these two?"

"Noooo!" Jesna shouted again.

At that moment—the nano-moment after Pete's curious fingers came to rest on the red buttons—the humming car began to vibrate like Mrs. Pilgrim's pressure cooker. I made a desperate leap through the air. The Pilgrims and Jesna became airborne just after me. We all landed in a head first dog-pile in the back seat of the car. I was the dog that was piled on. I was under all the Pilgrims on the back floor board. Everyone else's bottom was high above its corresponding head as bright colors began to explode all around.

"Yeee-Haw!" Pete cried as he was providing us with a bottom's-eye view of time travel—at breakneck speed.

Jesna was the first to disentangle herself from the monkey-fist knot we had created. She dove over into the front seat and used her small hips as battering rams to grab the controls.

"Hey!" Pete exclaimed from his new seat on the floor. "That hurt my…"

"Shhh!" Mr Pilgrim shouted from the back seat as he was dislodging my front paws from his mouth. "You haven't felt hurt yet. If I can just get up there and get you in a spanking position…."

I threw my paws over the front seat in time to see that Jesna was desperately punching buttons and pulling levers. The intensity of her work had taken on a life and death seriousness.

"Hey, what's the big deal?" Pete said. "I just wanted to go for a little spin around the block. I thought I might ask Jesus if he wanted to come along."

"Oh, my goodness!" Jesna exclaimed just as we burst through the tunnel of spinning colors.

All four Pilgrims let out a chorus of blood-curdling screams. The "big deal" was racing right toward us. The only question left was whether we would smash into a thousand bits, or drown.

(To be continued in *The Bible Ride*, Book 2.)

FAMILY DISCUSSION

1. What do you suppose it would feel like to have a hard, un-leavened heart?

2. What does it feel like to have soft, God-Spirit-filled heart?

ENDNOTES

Except where otherwise noted, all Scripture is quoted from *The Message,* © Eugene H. Peterson 1993, 1994, 1995.

Scene	*Note*	
1	1.	From Matthew 1:1; Mark 1:1; Luke 1:1-4; John 1:1-18.
	2.	John 1:1-13.
2	3.	From Luke 1:5-25.
3	4.	From Luke 1:26-38.
	5.	Luke 1:26-38.
4	6.	From Luke 1:39-56.
	7.	Luke 1:46-55.
5	8.	From Luke 1:57-80.
	9.	Luke 1:68, 76-79.
6	10.	From Matthew 1:2-17; Luke 3:23-38.
7	11.	From Matthew 1:18-25; Luke 2:1-7.
8	12.	From Matthew 2:1-12; Luke 2:8-20.
	13.	Luke 2:10, 12, 14.
	14.	From Matthew 2:6.
9	15.	From Luke 2:21-38.
10	16.	From Matthew 2:13-21.
	17.	Luke 2:29-32.
11	18.	From Matthew 2:22-23; Luke 2:39-40.
12	19.	From Luke 2:41-52.
	20.	Luke 2:49.
13	21.	From Matthew 3:1-6; Mark 1:2-6; Luke 3:1-6; John 1:19-23.
14	22.	From Matthew 3:7-10; Luke 3:7-9.
	23.	Matthew 3:7-9.
15	24.	From Luke 3:10-14.
	25.	Luke 3:10-11.

16 . . . . 26.	From Matthew 3:11-12; Mark 1:7-8; Luke 3:15-18; John 1:24-28.
27.	Matthew 3:11-12.
17 . . . . .28.	From Matthew 3:13-17; Mark 1:9-11; Luke 3:21-22; John 1:29-34.
29.	Matthew 3:17.
18 . . . . .30.	From Matthew 14:3-4; Mark 6:17-18; Luke 3:19-20.
31.	Matthew 3:15.
19 . . . . .32.	From Matthew 1:1-17; Luke 3:23-38.
20 . . . . .33.	From Matthew 4:1-11; Mark 1:12-13; Luke 4:1-13.
34.	Matthew 4:3-10.
21 . . . . .35.	From Matthew 4:18-22; Mark 1:16-20; Luke 5:1-11; John 1:35-56.
36.	Luke 5:4-10.
22 . . . . .37.	From John 2:1-11.
23 . . . . .38.	From John 2:12.
24 . . . . .39.	From John 2:13.
25 . . . . .40.	From Matthew 21:12-13; Mark 11:15-17; Luke 19:45-46; John 2:14-22.
41.	John 2:16-20.
26 . . . . .42.	From John 2:23-25.
27 . . . . .43.	From John 3:1-21.
44.	John 3:2-8.
45.	John 3:16.
28 . . . . .46.	From John 3:22.
29 . . . . .47.	From John 3:23-36.
48.	John 3:26-36.
30 . . . . .49.	From Matthew 4:12; Mark 1:14a; Luke 4:14a; John 4:1-30.
31 . . . . .50.	From John 4:4-42.
51.	John 4:9-26.
32 . . . . .52.	From Matthew 13:53-58; Mark 6:1-6a; Luke 4:16-30; John 7:15; 6:42; 4:44; 10:39.
53.	Luke 4:18-19.

33 . . . . .54.   From Luke 4:25-30.
34 . . . . .55.   From Mark 1:23-28; Luke 4:33-37.
            56.   Mark 1:22, 24.
            57.   Luke 4:36.
35 . . . . .58.   From Matthew 8:14-15; Mark 1:29-31;
                 Luke 4:38-39.
36 . . . . .59.   From Matthew 8:16-17; Mark 1:32-34;
                 Luke 4:40-41.
37 . . . . .60.   From Mark 1:35-38; Luke 4:42-43.
38 . . . . .61.   From Matthew 8:1-4; Mark 1:40-45;
                 Luke 5:12-16.
            62.   Mark 1:44.
39 . . . . .63.   From Matthew 9:1-8; Mark 2:1-2;
                 Luke 5:17-26; John 5:1-7, 8-9.
            64.   Mark 2:5.
            65.   Mark 2:8-9.
40 . . . . .66.   From Matthew 9:9-13; Mark 2:13-17;
                 Luke 5:27-32.
            67.   Matthew 9:12-13.
41 . . . . .68.   From Matthew 9:14-17; Mark 2:18-22;
                 Luke 5:33-39; John 3:29-30.
            69.   Matthew 9:14-17.
42 . . . . .70.   From Matthew 12:1-8; Mark 2:23-28;
                 Luke 6:1-5.
            71.   Matthew 12:3-7.
43 . . . . .72.   From Matthew 12:9-14; Mark 3:1-6;
                 Luke 6:6-11.
            73.   Mark 3:4.
44 . . . . .74.   From Matthew 4:24-25; 12:15-16;
                 Mark 3:7-12; Luke 6:17-19.
45 . . . . .75.   From Matthew 10:1-4; Mark 3:13-19a;
                 Luke 6:12-16.
46 . . . . .76.   From Matthew 4:24-5:2; Mark 3:7-13a;
                 Luke 6:17-20a.
            77.   Matthew 5:3-10.

47 . . . . 78. From Matthew 5:13; 5:14-16; Mark 9:49-50;
                    4:21; Luke 14:34-35; 8:16; John 8:12.
            79. Matthew 5:13, RSV.
48 . . . . 80. From Matthew 5:17-20; Mark 13:31;
                    Luke 16:16-17.
            81. Matthew 5:17-20, RSV.
49 . . . . 82. From Matthew 5:21-26; Mark 11:25;
                    Luke 12:57-59.
            83. Matthew 5:21-24.
50 . . . . 84. From Matthew 5:27-32; Mark 9:43-48;
                    Luke 16:18.
            85. Matthew 5:29-30.
51 . . . . 86. From Matthew 5:33-37.
            87. Matthew 5:33-37, RSV.
52 . . . . 88. From Matthew 5:38-48; Luke 6:29-30;
                    6:27-28; 32-36.
            89. Matthew 5:38-44.
            90. Matthew 5:48.
53 . . . . 91. From Matthew 6:1-4.
            92. Matthew 6:1-4.
54 . . . . 93. From Matthew 6:5-15; Mark 11:25[26];
                    Luke 11:1-4.
            94. Matthew 6:9-13, RSV2.
            95. Matthew 6:13.
55 . . . . 96. From Matthew 6:19-24; Luke 12:33-34;
                    11:34-36; 16:13.
            97. Matthew 6:19-24.
            98. George MacDonald, *Lilith* (Grand Rapids,
                    Mich.: Eerdmans, 1981), 64-67.
56 . . . . 99. From Matthew 6:25-34; Luke 12:12-32.
           100. Matthew 6:25-32; Luke 12:32.
57 . . . . .101. From Matthew 7:1-5; Mark 4:24-25;
                    Luke 6:37-42; John 7:53-8:11.
           102. Luke 6:37-38.
           103. Luke 6:41-42, RSV2.

58 . . . . .104. From Matthew 7:7-11; Luke 11:9-13;
John 16:24; 14:13-14; 15:7.

105. Matthew 7:7-11.

59 . . . . .106. From Matthew 7:12; Luke 6:31.

107. Matthew 7:12.

60 . . . . .108. From Matthew 7:13-27; Luke 13:23-27;
6:43-49.

109. Matthew 7:13-27.

61 . . . . .110. From Matthew 8:5-13; Mark 2:1; 7:30;
Luke 7:1-10; John 4:46b-57.

62 . . . . .111. From Luke 7:11-17.

63 . . . . .112. From Matthew 8:18-22; Mark 4:35;
Luke 9:57-62.

113. Luke 9:62.

64 . . . . .114. From Matthew 8:23-27; Mark 4:35-41;
Luke 8:22-25.

65 . . . . .115. From Matthew 8:28-34; Mark 5:1-20;
Luke 8:26-39.

116. Mark 5:7.

66 . . . . .117. From Matthew 9:18-23; Mark 5:21-34;
Luke 8:40-48.

118. Mark 5:34.

67 . . . . .119. From Matthew 9:23-26; Mark 5:35-43;
Luke 8:49-56.

120. Mark 5:39b, RSV.

68 . . . . .121. From Matthew 9:32-34; Mark 3:22;
Luke 11:14-15.

69 . . . . .122. From Matthew 9:35-38; Mark 6:6b; 6:34;
Luke 8:1; 10:2; John 4:35.

70 . . . . .123. From Matthew 10:17-25; Mark 13:9-13;
Luke 12:11-12; 6:40; 21:12-19;
John 13:16.

124. Matthew 10:5-25.

71 . . . . .125. From Matthew 10:26-33; Luke 12:2-9.

126. Matthew 10:28-31.

72 . . . . .127. From Matthew 10:37-42; Mark 9:41;
                          Luke 14:25-27; 10:16; 17:33; John 12:25;
                          13:20.
          128. Matthew 10:38-39.
73 . . . . .129. From Matthew 11:2-6; Luke 7:18-23.
74 . . . . .130. From Matthew 11:4-19; Mark 1:2;
                          Luke 7:24-35.
          131. Luke 7:22.
75 . . . . .132. From Matthew 11:28-30.
          133. Matthew 11:28-30.
          134. Matthew 11:30b.
76 . . . . .135. From Matthew 26:6-13; Mark 14:3-9;
                          Luke 7:36-50; John 12:1-8.
77 . . . . .136. From Matthew 9:35; Mark 6:6b; 16:9;
                          Luke 8:1-3.
78 . . . . .137. From Matthew 12:22-30; 9:32-34;
                          Mark 3:22-27; Luke 11:14-15, 17-23;
                          John 7:20; 10:20; 8:48, 52.
          138. Luke 11:17b-20.
79 . . . . .139. From Matthew 12:31-37; 7:16-20;
                          Mark 3:28-30; Luke 12:10; 6:43-45.
          140. Matthew 12:31-33.
80 . . . . .141. From Matthew 12:38-42; 16:1-2a; Mark
                          8:11-12; Luke 11:16, 29-32; John 6:30.
          142. Matthew 12:39-40.
81 . . . . .143. From Matthew 12:43-45; Luke 11:24-26.
          144. Matthew 12:43-45a.
82 . . . . .145. From Matthew 12:46-50; Mark 3:31-35;
                          Luke 8:19-21; John 15:14.
          146. Matthew 12:50.
83 . . . . .147. From Matthew 13:1-9; Mark 4:1-9;
                          Luke 8:4-8.
          148. Mark 4:3-8.
84 . . . . .149. From Matthew 13:10-17; 25:29; Mark
                          4:10-12; 4:25; Luke 8:9-10, 18b; John
                          9:39; 12:37-40.

85 . . . . .150. From Matthew 13:18-23; Mark 4:13-20;
                         Luke 8:11-15.
         151. Matthew 5:15; 10:26; Mark 4:21-25;
               Luke 8:16-18.
86 . . . . .152. From Matthew 5:15; 10:26; Mark 4:21-25;
                         Luke 8:16-18.
         153. Mark 4:24-25, RSV.
87 . . . . .154. From Mark 4:26-29.
         155. Mark 4:26-29.
88 . . . . .156. From Matthew 13:24-30.
         157. Matthew 13:24-30.
89 . . . . .158. From Matthew 13:31-32; Mark 4:30-32;
                         Luke 13:18-19.
         159. Mark 4:31-32, RSV.
90 . . . . .160. From Matthew 13:33; Luke 13:20-21.
         161. Matthew 13:35.
         162. Luke 13:20-21, RSV.
         163. Matthew 13:37-39.